D-

Enjoy the jou...

with lov...

[signature]

Testimonials

Inspiring, insightful, invaluable! Awaken and Grow is a deeply meaningful, step-by-step practical spiritual guide that teaches readers how to "merge the doing of our bodies with the being of our Spirit". Christine Agro's extensive experience, powerful insights, tools, exercises, case studies and personal stories empower the reader to learn, heal, and grow victoriously and gloriously in alignment with our truth, power and internal support system. Christine further supports our spiritual transformation powerfully with an amazing "Awaken & Grow" Resource Bundle of "doing" as a bonus, making it easier than ever to integrate and activate positive shifts in our life from chaos and indecision to simplicity and flow. If you're ready to be the captain of your own ship and create real change, this book is for you!

- Marlene Elizabeth, International Best-Selling Author, MONEYWINGS™

As a business owner it's important to grow yourself as much as it is to grow your business. Awaken & Grow: A Practical Guide For Your Spiritual Journey offers insight and guidance for personal growth that an entrepreneur can apply to their business growth as well.

-Monica Shah, 7 Figure Business Coach, CEO Revenue Breakthrough

Christine Agro is the Elon Musk of spiritual excavation, healing and enlightenment. Christine is a maverick; using her extraordinary gifts, gathering her own information, she creates her own tools and facilitates healing processes unlike any other teacher I have encountered. The methods are simple, yet the effects are tremendous and the information profound. This book holds answers and solutions for every level of seeker from any part of the globe. I am excited for everyone who chooses to read it.

- Divya Chandra, founder of
The Women of India Summit

Christine's approach is warm and wise—her writing plays the role of guide and companion to whatever personal journey you may be embarking on.

-Nicole Centeno, Founder of Splendid Spoon

Awaken
& GROW

A PRACTICAL
GUIDE FOR YOUR
SPIRITUAL JOURNEY

Christine Agro

Haldi Press
Arlington, New York

Awaken & Grow
A Practical Guide For Your Spiritual Journey
Christine Agro
Haldi Press

Published by Haldi Press, Pleasant Valley, NY
Copyright ©2018 Christine Agro
All rights reserved.

Book Design: www.DavisCreative.com

Library of Congress Cataloging-in-Publication Data

Library of Congress Control Number: 2018911759

Christine Agro

Awaken & Grow: A Practical Guide For Your Spiritual Journey

    1. SEL032000 SELF-HELP / Spiritual 2. OCC019000 BODY,

        MIND & SPIRIT / Inspiration & Personal Growth

    Hardcover ISBN: 978-0-9826814-8-0

    Paperback ISBN: 978-0-692-03583-2

    E-Book ISBN: 978-1-7328268-0-9

Publication Year: 2018

Contents

Dedication

To all the brilliant points of light
stepping into their Awakened life,
thank you for your adventurous nature,
your courageous heart and
your willingness to dig deep.
Your learning, healing and growth
move the collective forward with each step you take.

Beyond your 'aha' moment
is something so profoundly wonderful.
It is your 'aha' life.

Acknowledgments

I am blessed to do this work and I feel this so greatly as I write this list of acknowledgments. Support is a curious word and there are many times and places that we don't feel as though we are supported. In looking at Support, I have come to realize that we conflate support with validation, appreciation, approval and acceptance. When we separate support from these other energies, we can see that support comes to us in many and varied ways.

My acknowledgments are to and for the beings in my life, some in body, some not, some know that they support me, others support me in ways unseen and unknown to them. What matters is these are the beings Spirit sends me to lift me when I feel like I can't continue, to help me discover insight and information that changes the lives of many, and who cheer me on and see the powerful mission to which I have said 'YES.' Some are my soul sisters, who whether near or far, in touch or out of touch, knowing they are a part of my life means that I am never, ever alone.

My heartfelt 'thank you' and deepest love goes to:

Caidin Agro, Chuck Agro, Trudy Viscardo, William Viscardo Sr., Patricia Yguado, Alex Yguado, Gertrude Rieker, Mamie Viscardo.

Maria Fregosi, Nan Bush, Bruce Weber, Grace Coddington, Salomé Galib, Sabina Hitchin, Ivy Slater Rachlin, Hope Moriki, Adriane Herman, Amanda Thornton, Lisa Merkle, Rebecca Hall Gruyter. Sara Willerson, Cathy Davis, Jack Davis.

Magnolia Mae, Pudge, Brew, Cassie, Miranda, Pebbles, Polly, Oscar, Polar Bear, Dream, Kodi, Hud, Bonito, River, Billie, Palomino, Rain, Skye, True.

Nadia Bizzotto, Grace Beggins, Amanda Proeber, Sandra Oberdorfer, Lori Voss-Furukawa, Linda Groszyk, Celeste Hartwell, Jillian Breitfeller, Amy Sophiella, Cappy Caporuscio

Mudita Chandra & Divya Chandra

Welcome!

Beyond the day to day exists a powerful space where we can create and manifest the life we desire. But so many of us never find it, let alone learn to navigate within it.

If you've ever had a moment where you just know there is something more, an AHA moment as it is often called, that is just the starting place of your awakening. Many people stop with the awareness and miss the powerful, life-changing world that lives just beyond the AHA, the world that turns your AHA moment into an AHA life!

Where most things in our life have an endpoint or a final outcome, our Spiritual awakening and growth are ever unfolding. With each step in our awareness, we realize there is so much more to living and to life. But until we have that awareness, we wouldn't even guess there was something beyond the life we know. It is the true amazingness and magic of conscious Spiritual growth, there is always another door to open, a deeper level of awareness, greater flow, and a greater ability to create what we truly want in our lives. It is a truly bottomless well.

Accessing the depths of that well is where I come in with Awaken & Grow: A Practical Guide For Your Spiritual Journey. I've been helping women step into awareness and into that world beyond for almost 20 years. I believe knowledge IS power.

It is only when we truly understand the process behind our Spiritual growth that our journey becomes our own. It is only when we understand the steps we go through as we Awaken & Grow, that we can explore the power and magic of being alive.

As a Spiritual Teacher and Clairvoyant, I get so excited when I uncover Universal Truths – those common threads that show up in the lives of my clients and students which shed light on the how, why and what-for of our lives.

The how: How we live as Spiritual Beings.

The why: Why are we experiencing our lives in the way that we are?

The what-for: What are we trying to learn?

To Awaken & Grow, it isn't enough to just gather the information. Our growth comes when we can see the information, understand what we are working on AND (most importantly) have the energetic tools to navigate the lesson – to learn and to heal.

Think of our Spiritual journey as a video game. Until you gather the insight and knowledge you need, until you learn the Spiritual lessons, until you learn and heal what you need to, you do not get to move to the next level of your awareness and of your life journey. You do not get the 'power-ups.' At each new level, there are new opportunities, new abilities, new ways to move through your life you couldn't have guessed or even comprehended until you found the key to unlock the next level.

Instead of real growth and real healing, I see so many people who are gatherers of knowledge, they take a class, they read a book, they gather information, but that's where their growth stops. The mental body is a real trickster. It can convince us that we are growing, when in fact, all we are doing is amassing information.

It is time for us to move beyond and start to do something with the awareness we are gathering.

The same is true for our meditation practices and our yoga practices. If within the practice you do not understand what you are working on Spiritually, or you do not see the things that happen in your life as the stepping stones to really understanding your own Spiritual journey, your meditation and yoga practices are modes of escaping, escaping the lessons that are actually trying to help you grow.

As children we are taught to push down or push away anything that makes us hurt, makes us sad, makes us uncomfortable. We are taught, consciously or unconsciously to stuff our emotions away, to push past our challenges, to overcome our obstacles but if we were able to understand why we felt hurt in the first place, or what those challenges were comprised of, or why those obstacles were in the way; we would learn the Spiritual lessons contained within those experiences and our lives would unfold in a different more greatly empowered way.

Without that awareness, we continue to experience similar dynamics, all with the Spiritual hope that we will learn the deeper lesson contained within these moments that are meant to help us grow as Spirit.

Few people know this though. Most of us move through our lives wondering why we have the challenges we do, pushing them down, shoving them into empty spaces within our being and hoping for the best as we move forward. Maybe we use meditation or yoga, or something else to help us manage our lives, to help us feel a deeper connection, but that deeper connection won't unlock the next level of your life because that connection is really only skin deep. It isn't true Spiritual growth.

Wouldn't it be great if you didn't have to hope for the best? Wouldn't it be great if you had the inside scoop on what exactly you are doing here as a Spiritual being? Wouldn't it be amazing if you knew energetic tools that could help you navigate your life lessons, create real healing and to grow as a Spiritual being and deepen your Spiritual connection?

All of this is the root of my work. It is the 'why' of why I am here. Over the years I have been shown by Spirit, various versions of who I am in the world—a guide, a teacher, a cheerleader; but my favorite is this one: a person who takes you from the unconscious side of life, walks you across the bridge sharing wisdom and tools as we walk and when you reach the other side—the conscious side, I set you off to continue walking on your path, empowered and enlightened.

People often ask me if I've always been clairvoyant and that question gives me pause. I have not always had the awareness and clarity I have now, but I have always had a connection to something more, something deeper; to the awareness that there is an answer to the question 'why are we here.' But it wasn't until my mid-30s when I began to unravel the how, why and what-for. It started by stepping into a Clairvoyant program which showed me how to look at my own life experiences, how to unravel the information those life experiences contained and how to work energetically to clear, transform or transmute the experiences so I could continue to grow in my conscious awareness.

Where many practices are rooted in a well-defined system, I believe these systems can actually stop us from learning and growing because the systems themselves so often do not grow. They stop at the place where the person who channeled them first experienced them. My work isn't like that. You could take the same program with me several times and the program would be different each time because whether I'm teaching, working with you one-to-one, speaking, or writing, I meet you in the moment and tap into your own Spirit and the energy of the collective consciousness to share what is needed in the moment.

To that end, the tools I share are always evolving as I look at where people are in their Spiritual unfolding. We, individually and collectively, are forever evolving. Our awareness is growing, our connection to our own Spiritual power is growing and so too our Spiritual growth processes and the tools we use to help us expand and grow should be in present time to serve us the most.

What To Expect

This book gives you a deep dive into the process of our Spiritual growth. What I have experienced with clients and students is this: it is in the understanding of our process where we can really step into true growth and keep moving through the higher levels of growth and awareness.

The general reaction to this information is 'ohhhhh, now I get it!' and at the same time a sense of, 'I already knew that, but I didn't know that.' We do already know this information, it is just buried in unconsciousness. My job is to help you peel away the unconscious layers.

While reading you may feel tired or sleepy, you may get distracted. This book isn't just a book. It is a Spiritual lesson. You will grow by reading this book. The energies which come up like the distraction and the falling asleep while reading, that's all normal. As we grow we hit energies and sometimes those energies do not want to shift, because if they do, you change and the whole 'game' changes. It can be helpful to make the conscious statement, 'Yes, I want to read this book. Yes, I want to take this step.' When we do this, we affirm that we are prepared to take a conscious step in our awareness.

The first part of this book, 'Awaken,' is all about the way in which we grow, the steps and process to awakening and what you can expect, or an explanation of what you have already experienced. The second part of this book 'Grow,' introduces you to the way in which we grow, the stages of our growth and what is required to grow. The third part of this book 'Putting it All Together' gives you tips, tools, exercises and insights to help you move more deeply into your Spiritual growth and deepen your Spiritual connection. You will also find throughout the book a collection of short stories from clients and students about their own Awakening. They share their first-hand experiences of stepping into awareness and how it has impacted their lives.

As my work is experiential and it is a bit difficult to turn reading about tools into action, I have put together the Awaken & Grow Bonus Package for you that gives you experiential opportunities to explore some of the tools and information I am sharing with you. Although you will have shifts by reading this book, there is so much more for you to experience when you actually do the work. So, I hope that you will move past adding another collection of information to your mental body reserves and join me for the experiential component of this book. You will find a list of everything included and a link to my Awaken & Grow Bonus Package at the end of the book.

If you want to reach out to me with questions or comments, I have a closed Facebook group that you can join and I'm happy to interact with you there. You'll find that link in the resource area as well.

I'm so excited to share this information with you and I hope that it supports you on your conscious Spiritual journey.

Thank you for being here!

xxxx

Chapter 1

*"A single event can awaken within us
a stranger totally unknown to us.
To live is to be slowly born."*
Antoine de Saint-Exupéry

What is an Awakening?

Awakenings come in many sizes and colors. Some are momentous occasions where the light bulb turns on and your whole life takes a right turn onto a path you didn't even see was there. These often throw you into a completely different direction than where you thought you were headed and come with a shedding off of those things, and even people, who are not in alignment with where you are headed. I call this a Grand Awakening. This grand awakening often comes with a sense that there must be more to life than what we are experiencing; a sense that there must be something more that we are supposed to be doing, need to be doing or ought to be doing. The awakening can also come with a sense of being called and sometimes there is no clear answer to exactly what it is that is calling us.

While other awakenings are small pops of awareness that many refer to as 'aha' moments, a moment when someone says something, does something or something happens that sheds light on your own journey and makes your life just that much clearer.

Some of us have one grand awakening and then experience a collection of aha moments, others of us will have several grand awakenings and a constellation of aha moments throughout our lives.

In part, your conscious experience is tied to how much you want to grow. If you're like me and many of my students, once you 'get it' you aren't happy with stopping there. You come to see your journey as the amazing and exciting gift that it is, rather than a collection of either random happenings, or in some cases a collection of frustrations and disappointments.

My first Grand Awakening happened in 1999 when I was 34 years old and living in Denver, Colorado. I worked on 17th Street but would park at the Boettcher Concert Hall and walk to work from there. On this particularly ordinary day, I was halfway to my office when it felt like a bolt of lightning struck me. I found myself questioning how I had gotten to this place in my life. Why was I doing the work I was doing? How did I come to live in Colorado? Why did I marry the person I married? I realized that every step had been unconscious. It is not that I had a bad life, quite the contrary, I really enjoyed my life, but in this moment, it was clear to me that I had been sleepwalking through my life and there was not only something more to life than what I was experiencing but something more that I was supposed to be doing.

By November of 1999, synchronicity had led me to a free energy healing clinic at The Inner Connection Institute in Denver. The work resonated so much with me that I signed up for their 6-week Psychic Awareness program and then went on to enroll in their 12-month Clairvoyant Program. It was in that program that I felt like I had come home. When we ignore or even deny a True part of ourselves, we walk around feeling incomplete but not even recognizing that we are incomplete. As I deepened into the work at The Inner Connection Institute, my inner Truth came forward, namely ownership of my Clairvoyance coupled with the tools and understanding to apply it in a way that could benefit not only the flow of my life but that of others.

In 2014, I had my second Grand Awakening. I had been working with students for six years, teaching women how to step into their own empowered, conscious lives. All of my students know that when we are in class if there is a concept that isn't resonating, or they aren't getting, it is possible the information is not for them or they might 'get it' during their own daily practice space. So, if this happens, students will sit and move energy while the class moves forward.

In this specific class, a student came into the class with energy activated. She was agitated energetically. I acknowledged the space she was in. I tried amusement because often that helps us shift, but the energy remained. As the class moved forward she got even more activated and began questioning the information. She didn't understand it, couldn't get it and demanded that I explain it to her and help her 'get it.' After presenting several ways of supporting her, I finally heard myself say, 'I don't have anything else for you.' I paused before moving forward with the class because I knew these words didn't come from me and they were not only for her, but they were for me as well.

This student and I reached the end of our Spiritual Agreement, but there was something in my statement for me. To back-track, a Spiritual Agreement is the energetic contract between two people or a group and the purpose of the agreement is learning, healing and growing. I find agreements really fascinating because our agreements range from one-to-one relationships to the agreement we have with all of the Spirits that are here on the planet right now. Ending an agreement follows the 'Cosmic Correction' methodology (More on this in a moment.) We get small messages that the agreement is over, that it doesn't serve us any more or that we are supposed to be doing something else. If we do not listen to those smaller messages, the messages get louder and louder until we end up with a huge blowout. Which is what happened in this class. It was like an energetic bomb went off.

Following up from the class, I reached out to the student and said, 'It looks like it is time for you to stop working with me.' She agreed, and we parted ways. For my part, I sat in meditation and received guidance looking for insight into the questions that were floating through my mind. 'What does this mean for me? What am I being asked to do?' And the answers came without a clear direction or outcome, but I knew, that should I not follow the insight, things would get difficult.

I was being asked to stop my work with others and focus on myself. Of course, 'focus on myself,' to me meant, 'Found The Church of Nature,' but in that regard, my teaching became not about the information I was channeling, but rather the information Nature had for us. What I experienced during this time was a syncing of the information I had been channeling since 1999 and what I came to understand as Universal Truths. In 2017, when Spirit said, 'ok, it is time to get back to work,' I was not only ready, I felt like I was emerging from a cocoon as a new glorious butterfly.

Here's the thing with this second Awakening, I employed everything that I had been teaching about living in alignment and following the threads of guidance and inspiration and my students were able to witness me following my inner guidance, while admittedly not knowing where it was taking me. As I closed down my online communities and completed the programs I had running, I followed the threads that were coming to me. I stepped into a landscape design program, honeybee guardianship, Permaculture, mandala making, mosaic work and started showing my artwork again. My students got to see the power in following the threads and saying 'yes' to our inner guidance as I was on a journey without a known purpose yet knowing there was a purpose. It was an incredible experience all around.

How Does An Awakening Happen?

What is a Grand Awakening, Really? And how do they come about?

A Grand Awakening is when we step out of the haze of our existence to realize that life as we have experienced it, as we have understood it, is an illusion, or just the tip of the iceberg of what being here is really all about. We have a sudden awareness that what we know and what we believe is untrue or that what we have been told limits us and restricts us from being full. It is a moment when we realize that we are only partially living and that there is something more beyond what we have experienced so far AND, we are compelled to discover what it is.

Grand Awakenings come about gradually, but most of the time, they feel like they came out of nowhere and they can feel like our world is falling apart. Awakening doesn't have to unfold this way, but for so many who travel their path without guidance or support, that's how their awakenings happen. There isn't a right way or a wrong way to awaken, but by understanding our Spiritual process, we can choose a simpler way.

Cosmic Corrections

A Cosmic Correction is an ultimate shift in our awareness and oftentimes feels like the rug has been pulled out from under you. It is a powerful moment, usually associated with some sort of life-altering happening like an accident or a death or an illness; a divorce or a job loss. Something that really shakes the foundation of life as you know it.

Cosmic Corrections do not happen out of the blue. Typically, they are the end result of quieter, more gentler messages. Spirit has been sending us quiet, gentle messages, asking us to pay attention and we brush them off like a pesky fly until one day Spirit sends a fly so large you can't brush it off. A Cosmic Correction is when something happens in our life that is so big and so life-changing, and its purpose is to put us on our path.

Some people feel it is God or the Universe that does the course correcting. After years of working with people, I'd say it is our own Spirit, but whatever you believe, Cosmic Corrections are the equivalent of an invisible hand stepping in and creating change.

I actually love cosmic corrections because, without them, we'd be wandering, or lingering in a place that doesn't help us accomplish what we wanted to experience this lifetime.

The thing with Cosmic Corrections is that they always start off gently and quietly with a little nudge that says 'hey, you aren't in the right place.' Because we are human, we can ignore the gentle quiet nudge and we carry on with whatever it was we were doing and however, it was that we were doing it.

Cosmic Corrections then proceed to get louder and louder, until they are so loud that you are simply compelled to listen and that is what so many of us experience. That loud, can't be ignored Cosmic Correction often comes in the form of a health crisis or a dramatic event of some sort; it is always something that is so loud that you just can't turn away from it. It makes you sit up and say, 'I should be doing something else.'

Avoiding the Cosmic Correction

You can't really avoid it altogether, but what you can do is recognize it right off the bat when it is that quiet, gentle nudge; when it is a whisper that you are not in the right place or doing the right thing or pursuing something that is not in alignment with who you are.

If you stop and take a moment to reflect you know when you are being asked to do things differently in your life. You have your own spidey sense that tingles when something isn't right in your life. The question is, how often do you listen? If you've been programmed to dismiss what you know (which primarily happens during our childhood,) you might be inclined to downplay that knowingness.

If you have been dismissing your knowingness, it is time to stop. It is time to dust off your finely tuned senses and start to listen to those messages that come through feelings, senses, and thoughts. Trust that if something doesn't 'feel' right to you, it probably isn't and start to look for solutions and options that will help you change your circumstances before your own Spirit forces you to make those changes.

Grand Awakenings can happen in every aspect of our life. We can have a health grand awakening that comes after we get sick or have a major accident. We 'wake-up' and realize that we need to take better care of ourselves. Or we can have a grand awakening in our professional life. We work ourselves to death and wake up one morning and all of sudden we see that all we have is our work. Maybe we've lost our family because of it, or never had one because of it; but whatever the awareness is, we wake up to the fact that work isn't everything.

Why Do We Have An Awakening?

Awakenings happen to help move us from living life unconsciously into living life with conscious awareness. They happen at a time when we are ready to take that step forward into a new way of seeing, being and living. The most fascinating thing is that when we are unconscious we have no idea that something more exists. We move through our days happy or not, satisfied, or not, but we take our lives as they show up. We may strive to do things differently, to achieve things, to create what we want, but we do it from unconsciousness. Much like the way I moved through my life before I had my first Awakening. I liked art so I went to art school. I showed my work, but I knew I didn't want to live the life of an artist, so I went back to school and got my MBA. I had worked in galleries and saw them close because they didn't have funding, which never made sense to me, so I specialized in Non-profit/Arts Management. I got a paying internship at a major art gallery and from there got hired as a Director of Development before I even graduated from the MBA program and my life rolled on. People would say I was always in the right place at the right time. Looking back, I can see that I was always guided. My life flowed all the way to Colorado and to my first Awakening. But I was unconscious to it all. I just kept putting one foot in front of the other. As I said already, it was a great life. But as soon as I had my Awakening, I realized how much more there was. I could see that all the things that had happened in my life were directed and were leading me to something and seeing this, I didn't want to just let my life 'happen' anymore. I wanted to understand how, why and for what reason my life flowed like it did.

So many people live their entire lives without reaching this moment. It doesn't make their lives wrong. But reaching this moment is a key part of our Spiritual Journey. When we incarnate the question from the beginning is will we or won't we lift the veil in this lifetime. If something has been nudging you to dig deeper, to take a step, to see what is in front of you and to explore your own how, why and for what, I can tell you that there is a life you can't imagine calling you and a life inviting you to step more deeply onto a path of conscious living. As we move forward in this book, you'll gain insight, guidance, and tools to help you say 'yes' to taking that step.

What Is The Process of Awakening?

Prior to a grand awakening, messages were coming—your blood pressure was creeping up, you weren't getting enough sleep, your partner kept asking you to be present; whatever it was, small messages, small requests to make changes until WHAM you wake-up and change is not an option anymore, change is happening.

Signs are an interesting thing. When I was at the beginning of my awakened road, I can remember seeing signs that reaffirmed different choices I was making. I would be considering a move and I would see the state I was thinking about moving to over and over again. Today, my Spirit works with me through numbers. I often see the same number combinations over and over. I use Doreen Virtue's Angel Numbers book to decipher them, but I could just as easily tap into my own intuition to know what the message is. I do love her channeled messages though, so I stick with hers. Why reinvent the wheel!

Signs come in many variations.

Let's talk about the different ways you can get guidance from your own Spirit, guidance that helps keep you on the right track, that helps affirm your choices. The important thing is to use signs as affirmations, not as crutches. We do not need a sign, but it is nice to get one. Also, the more you recognize and accept the messages, the more they will come.

How Do You Know It Is a Message?

A divinely inspired message is like having a prophetic dream versus a regular dream. There is something different in the quality of the experience. For me, my prophetic dreams have a clarity that my other dreams do not have. They are grounded in reality, there isn't any of the disjointedness that exists in my regular dreams—nothing is out of place and I do not find myself in my dream wondering why someone or something is doing what it is doing or wearing what they are wearing. In fact, if you experience prophetic dreams, that is in itself a form of receiving messages.

A message regardless of how it comes to you will grab your attention. It says, 'hey, I'm talking to you.' When I lived in Colorado, I did what one is told not to do. I hiked by myself, or with one of my dogs (not alone in my mind.) I was out hiking one day, and I got turned around. I couldn't find the trail. I had a moment of panic and then let it go and simply asked for help. I said, 'I'm a bit lost, can I get some help.' A few minutes later a Magpie came and sat on a tree and started cawing. I started walking in one direction and the Magpie put up a good fuss. I stopped walking and it stopped fussing. I did it again and it fussed some more. I stopped, it stopped. I finally looked up at it and said, 'are you talking to me?' and it cawed back to me and flew to a tree branch in the opposite direction I had been heading. I figured, 'ok, I asked for help. Here I go,' and I followed it. It continued to fly from tree to tree and I followed along and then I saw it, the trailhead. It had led me to the trailhead.

Signs often have an 'otherworldly' sense to them. That 'are you talking to me?' sense. You see them or hear them, and you just know, 'that was meant for me.' The more you trust that, the more you'll receive messages.

I've put together just a few ways that messages can come to us:

Numbers

With digital clocks, odometers, gas pumps, cash registers and more, it is really easy to set up direct communication with your Spirit for affirmation and guidance. As I already noted, I love Doreen Virtue's Angel Numbers app to help you decipher the messages and meaning. But to get you started here are just a few things I know about different numbers: 8s are about abundance and flow of prosperity. I often see 808 which for me has come to be connected to my belief in living with an open heart and an open hand, open to both giving and receiving. Think of 8 as a symbol of infinity, of endless possibility and unlimited abundance.

Anything with a 1 in it is connected to Spirit, Spiritual guidance, and Spiritual direction. 11:11 means 'you're right on track.' with a 5 in it means change is happening or change is coming. Anything with a 4 is a reassurance that you have been heard, you are supported, and help is being provided.

However, here's the rub: if you aren't open to the help, you're going to think there is no support. Help comes in so many ways, and often in ways that we do not see, but typically help doesn't come the way you think it should. When you ask for support, guidance, insight, direction—you have to be open to receiving it. Just like I was when I was hiking. Our mental body might think that when we asked for help we would find a trail guide, or someone would happen along, for most, the thought that a bird would show up and guide us is something that could be easily missed. We must be open to receive if we are asking for help.

Images and Words and Songs

Just like recurring numbers, images and words can bring us messages. Maybe you are hyper-aware of the word 'patience' and it constantly pops up around you. You hear it in conversations, you see people either being patient or not having patience, you see examples in books and movies, the notion of patience is highlighted. There's a message there.

People

I love it when messages pop up through people. Sometimes it is the reappearance of someone I haven't seen in years and they pop in and then they are gone again. Pay attention to your interactions. What are they talking about, what does their presence bring up for you? Within your encounter is bound to be a message. In other cases, sometimes the people around us bring us direct messages without even knowing it.

My Dad passed away suddenly in 2008. It was emotionally challenging, even with what I know Spiritually about life and death. I found myself wondering, 'was my dad proud of me?' It was an odd thing for me to wonder because, in my heart, I knew that he was. Over the course of the next several months after his passing, people would, out of nowhere, say 'your dad was proud of you.' I heard it from people I barely knew, from clients, from friends, it was said to me over and over and then I realized, it was my father speaking to me. I didn't need to know that he was proud of me, but he wanted me to know, so he worked through people to make sure I knew. After I realized that this was a message from my father, I started to pay attention to the way in which this phrase was said. Inevitably the person speaking seemed to not know why they said it. One even remarked, after saying it, 'I don't know why I just said that.' All I could think was 'thanks, Dad!'

Animals

Animals both wild and domestic have strong agreements with humanity to help us do our learning, healing and growing. If you are open to working with animal messengers they will come to you as a form of guidance, insight, and direction. When I first started working with Animal Messengers, it was a friend who introduced me to them. I would call her and say, 'I saw a rabbit, what did it mean?' I was so fascinated by the way in which these messages were coming, I was often reaching out to her to find out what message was being offered. She finally said to me, 'get Ted Andrews book, Animal Speak.' What a great and helpful resource this is. He goes through different animals, birds, and even some insects and offers what each brings as a messenger.

The more you work with messages, be it from animals or numbers or words or images, you will develop your own understanding of the insight they share. What you gather from the messages you receive may be in alignment with a book or an oracle deck or it might not. What you need to know is that the messages will come to you in the way you can have and it is important as you deepen your connection to messages, that you honor your own intuition of what the messages mean.

Deja' Vu All Over Again

How many times are you going to have the same lesson? Didn't you already deal with that? These are thoughts that go through anyone's mind who is working on growing. It is human nature to think that because we are experiencing what seems like the same lesson, that we are having to repeat it or do it again, or even that we have somehow gone backward in our growth but more often than not, what you are actually dealing with is a deeper layer of the same lesson. There are some cases where the same experience is actually presenting a different lesson. This happened to me. For many years public speaking was excruciating for me. I would all but hyperventilate when I spoke in public. The energy in my body would vibrate so intensely my entire body would shake. I worked for years on the lesson of being seen—peeling away layers of wounding and fear, but yet still the lesson persisted. I never gave up on speaking because I knew it was part of my purpose to share what I know. Then one day, I saw it. I was looking at the energy that comes up when I would speak and there it was. It wasn't about 'being seen' or at least not anymore. The remaining piece was about having my truth accepted. And here's the thing about that, it doesn't matter to me if someone accepts what I have to say. I know as Spiritual Beings we all learn in the way that is right for us. If someone doesn't accept what I have to say, it means they've ruled out one possible option, or maybe, something I say lights up something that they can heal, but whatever the reason, accept or do not accept, it is all important. Once I saw that this is what the energy was wrapped around, it was easy to let it go.

There are so many layers and levels to our growth. I've laid out everything for you here that I know about it to-date. You do not need to know everything or remember everything to move forward in your own awakened state. What you read here will come back to you when the time is right. I encourage you to start from where you are, be open to the messages that come, follow the guidance and see where it leads you.

AHAs

Did you have any Ahas or questions from this chapter?

Write them here and then join me over at my Awaken & Grow FB Group and share them. Your Aha or your question may help someone else (almost always does!) www.facebook.com/groups/awakenandgrow

Awaken & Grow Stories

Jillian Rose, *Author of*
Carry The Moon Across The Sky

My awakening process was not gentle. It came on slowly and then all at once. Flooding me. Shaking my foundation. It was an imperative. An expansive and fast-moving trajectory toward the light.

Before my awakening, I was afraid. I say this in such a general way, because it was truly an overarching force in my life. It coated everything in its slow weight. Because of this, my I was always moving through life in an uphill way. Fighting tides, losing momentum, and staying small to protect myself.

I always felt it, however. When I looked up at the stars, across the ocean, or into the colors of a setting sun—the beauty of this world that I for some reason was not allowing myself to embrace. That I could appreciate but couldn't be a part of. Always separate, but always believing in something more. An ethereal magic that was one with this sky, but grounded with every root, every footstep, and every breath.

Through my work in meditation with Christine Agro, my incredible classmates and our learnings and tools, and this certain intangible drive that kept pushing me ahead, I started to wake up. I understood the power of intention, awareness, intuition, and my own Spirit. I learned to work with my energy—to look at it, shift it, move it out, and learn from the messages it brought me. And then, these learnings turned into something more tangible. Something that I could have never imagined. I started to shift in a way that felt beyond conscious choice (it was my choice—it just felt that way). My Spirit started to take the lead, and with it, everything changed. I felt it coursing through my body in a physical way. I felt it in my heart. I saw my place in this vast Universe. I spoke to a force beyond myself—though, simultaneously, housed within. And though I was terribly afraid at first, soon, my walls broke down. And everything became even more beautiful.

Now, I live my life in a different way. That is not to say I am never afraid, or sad, or angry. I am human, after all, and I wouldn't want it any other way. But with my heightened awareness and a higher voice to follow, I can learn from these things, and when it is right, access the power to change them. Life will never be the same. It can't. Once you see the light in your heart, you just know—and the flame can never go out.

Chapter 2

'Who we are unawakened is just
the tip of the iceberg of who we can be,
what we can do and
what we can have once we Awaken.'
Christine Agro

Why are We Here?

This is a question that humanity has asked throughout the ages. For some the answer rests in religion, for others, the answer is about what we do, and still, for others, it is about who we are and how we show up in the world and identifying a meaningful purpose.

For me, it is simple. We are here to learn, heal and grow as Spiritual Beings.

I've come to this simple, paired down understanding by looking at the layers of our lives. We have many layers to our lives that include who we are, how we are seen, what we do in the world, what family, race or religion we belong to and what we are passionate about but underneath all of that, at the core, is the nut of why we are here. To learn. To heal. To grow.

What are we doing and why are we doing it? Why in the grand scheme of things are we all here? In order to understand this fully, we need to zoom out and look at the big picture 'WHY.' For me, that means looking at the Collective Consciousness. The Collective Consciousness is the sum total of all energies, all beings. If you are religious, you may see this as GOD, but I see GOD as a piece of The Collective energy, as a part of what makes up the whole. The Collective is a fascinating place to journey into (and if you are interested, as part of the Awaken & Grow Bonus Pack, I've included a guided meditation to help you explore it. The link to the Bonus Pack is at the back of the book.) The Collective Consciousness is a space where we can be all of it, a piece it, move through it and be an observer to it. It is made up of all Spiritual Beings. Some Beings can stand on their own or are individuated and others are a part of the total energy and act within it. It is called The Collective Consciousness because it is the sum total of the experiences of all lifetimes and within all of that rests the architecture of this grand game which is, 'can we evolve to the place where we can live fully as Spirit with a body?' Meaning, can we step into conscious awareness and recognize that we are Spirit first (The Collective Consciousness) and that our bodies are vehicles for the power of our Spiritual essence? That's the whole experiment.

Therefore, for each of us, our primary purpose is to learn, heal and grow in order to see if we can reach an aligned state of being in any given lifetime. Each time we try, we move the collective forward. We learn what works, what doesn't work, what sets us back and what moves us forward. In order to evolve The Collective Consciousness, we have come in and lived lives of piety and of debauchery. We have been the predator and the prey. We have been poor and rich. We have been successful and we have failed. We have had rich relationships and we have lived lives of emptiness and loneliness. Each time we incarnate we learn something new about what it means to be in a physical body and about what it takes to live fully as Spirit and each time we incarnate, we advance the Collective Consciousness.

Beyond being here to learn, heal and grow; everything else we do in a lifetime is a bonus. However, when we are still in our unconscious state we forget this and instead of the learning, healing and growing being our focus, we get off track and who we are and what we do and what we have drives us. It is our mind and our ego and sometimes our physical body that pushes us forward with 'doing.' Have you heard the expression we are human beings, not human doings? Although a catchy phrase, I find this to be one of those sayings that sounds good, but people do not really understand or know what it means. In my experience, it is interpreted as the difference between what you do and who you are.

I did a quick check-in on my Awaken & Grow Facebook group and here are some of the ways people describe 'Human Doing Vs Human Being.'

- "How you are" is important rather than what you act upon
- Your value or worth does not lie in how much you do or accomplish.
- Human "doing" is getting your kids to school, doing the dishes, doing your job well. Human "being" means being present, being compassionate, being here in this moment. So "being" is encompassing the attribute, "doing" is just the busy work of it.

You can see that these explanations, where not wrong, all have actions as comparisons. What you do versus who you are or how you are.

I see this as our unconscious understanding. It is our understanding because we can't know there is something more if we aren't aware of it. But I do see something more, something deeper in this saying and when this happens, I like to first, go to the definitions of words and then move from there because oftentimes, just in reading the definition you will have an 'aha.'

From Webster's Dictionary:

Doing: performance, performing, carrying out, execution, implementation, implementing, achievement, accomplishment, realization, completion;

Being: existence; the nature or essence of a person.

The words 'Human Doing' call attention to the truth that when we live unconsciously it is our mind, body, emotions, and ego that propel us forward. We are constantly in the act of doing, of trying to get somewhere, of trying to be someone. When we live unconsciously, it is this act of 'doing' that moves us from point A to point B in our life without really knowing how we got there.

The words 'Human Being' ask us to consider, not the 'how' but rather the true nature or essence of who we are and to consider why we are here. Denoting that we are Human Beings is asking us to wake up to the truth that we are not our bodies. We are the essence. We are Spirit.

At the root of this is: the 'why' of why we are here gets lost until we awaken.

It gets lost in our mental body searching for understanding and meaning when all the while, our Spirit knows the answers.

It gets lost in our ego feeling like it needs to do something or be something when all the while, our Spirit knows what we are here to do.

Our journey is about the experiences we have and the learning that comes from those experiences.

It is about the growth that we experience.

It is about opening up to greater clarity.

It is about clearing the clutter and creating room for our Spirit to live fully within our body.

It is about the ever-unfolding possibility of seeing more, having more and being more.

Why Don't We Come In Awakened?

Why do we awaken in the first place? Why don't we just come in with awareness?

I go back to the point that the whole purpose is to see if we can get to the place where we can merge the doing of our bodies with the being of our Spirit. I believe we did once come in fully awakened. These were the ancient cities of Lemuria and Atlantis, but what was learned was that the mind, the ego, and emotions, if not cultivated to handle the power of Spirit, can result in the total misuse of our inherent Spiritual power. Thus, we have this journey to test us every step of the way and see if we are ready for the full power of our Spiritual Being channeling through our physical bodies.

In essence, living fully connected and having access to our Spiritual power is a gift that must be earned and our journey from unconscious to awakened is the test.

AHAs

Did you have any Ahas or questions from this chapter?

Write them here and then join me over at my Awaken & Grow FB Group and share them. Your Aha or your question may help someone else (almost always does!) www.facebook.com/groups/awakenandgrow

Chapter 3

*"Life is really simple,
but men insist on making it complicated."*
—Confucius

What Is Our
Spiritual Journey Like?

I hosted a six-day on-line Summit called 'Step Up & Step In' and I interviewed 18 experts from a myriad of fields—business, brand identity, law of attraction, mindfulness, health, and fitness and even healthy eating. I asked each expert the same question, 'were you called to step up & step in and did you listen?' The answer was a resounding 'yes, I was, and no, I did not listen initially.' Granted, not listening is a big part of our growth process—everything that happens when we do not listen to the quiet, gentle nudges from Spirit is a part of our learning, healing and growing. Those nudges get louder and louder until we finally can no longer ignore them.

We so often do not listen until the message gets really loud and really uncomfortable. It would be great if we just listened when the nudges were quiet and gentle and that's what you are going to get throughout this book: the insight and the tools to help you recognize those first nudges and the courage to listen to what those nudges are telling you.

There are so many things that stop us from listening and taking a step and they are all connected to what we are here to learn: fear—of anything or everything, uncertainty or a need to know where you are going before you get there, control, expectation, responsibility, perfection—each of these things is connected to your own life lessons.

I was working with a woman who was defending her project for her thesis and her first defense was shot down. She said to me, 'I feel like my life is out of my control.' When I asked, 'how so,' she explained that the power over what happens in her life is out of her own hands. She is dependent upon whether her project is accepted, whether she receives funding and that she has no control over the outcome of those decisions. In the mindset she was in, the outcome of her life was sitting in a passive dynamic. We shifted this by looking at all of the things that she could do to help create what she wants; the ways she could work the energy around the situation; connect and communicate Spiritually with those who are in the seat of deciding and most importantly, standing in her certainty and turning her inner fire up to 'make it happen.' Much of the Ph.D. program is a challenge to see if you truly believe what you believe, know what you know and are prepared to fight for it. Notice the parallel here to our Life Journey. We are challenged in our growth to see if we have the full power of our Spiritual Being.

Taking the step, whatever that step may be; leaving a relationship, changing jobs, enrolling in school or a program, whatever that step is will bring up many opportunities for you to learn your life lessons because the step is connected to your deeper growth.

In part, this dynamic is because our unconscious way of learning is through challenge and adversity. It is these two things that push us to grow when we live life unconsciously. The beauty is, we do not have to learn through adversity once we Awaken. That is why waking up creates a state of flow in our lives. I'm going to talk a lot about this as we move on in the book, but before we get there, it will be helpful for you to understand some of the 'how and why' in the ways that we learn. Helpful, because it is good to know where we come from and where we are going and also good to know because as you step into a different way of living your life, you will be able to understand where others are in their own journey.

Sometimes writing about Spiritual truths and Spiritual information is a bit like which came first 'the chicken or the egg.' On the Spirit plane, time and space are not linear, so oftentimes things occur simultaneously. But we can't speak about concepts simultaneously.

That's a bit of the case with our stages of awareness and the way in which we learn. I initially began this section with Spiritual Learning but kept needing to touch on the stages of awareness while doing so. So, I've put the stages first, although, in writing it, I keep feeling inclined to speak about the way in which we learn. With that, as we move through this information, keep that in mind. If something needs more explanation, trust that it will be revealed as we move along with the information. You can also make a note of your question, just in case you do not find clarity further along in the book and then you can reach out to me directly for an answer.

Stages of Awareness

It was in animals that I first recognized our stages of awareness. Sometimes Spiritual truths show up much more simply with our animal friends than with humans. We are so much more complicated, and that's not really a compliment. Animals have a simplicity to their process because they do not get caught up in their ego or their minds like we do. But once I saw the stages of awareness in animals, these easily translated to people.

I want to preface this information with this—the stages of awareness are not like stages of growth or linear in any way. We do not start out in one stage with the expectation we will reach another. Our growth is directly related to how we move through the world, what we say 'yes' to, the healing we experience and the Spiritual agreements we have.

Unconscious

When we are unconscious we move through our lives unaware that there is anything beyond what exists.

Someone in this state questions nothing and accepts everything as it is. They roll along never wondering why things happen or considering if there is another way. Their lives usually flow through different levels from ease to tragedy to ease, but through each life experience, the person simply experiences it at face value and moves on. There is no conscious awareness of life lessons, of spiritual growth, of searching for something more.

Someone who is unconscious is unaware of anything beyond the physical reality. They may or may not believe in a 'higher power' but if they do, it is in a way to provide comfort and reassurance that there is something after this life.

When I've seen this stage in dogs they are typically difficult to train, have no awareness of cause and effect and tend to be very physical body oriented—meaning, their awareness is based in their day-to-day experience. They are often happy and content with what is.

Young Children are sometimes unconscious as well. The world revolves around them and they have no awareness of cause and effect or that their actions may impact someone else. Their focus is on their needs and how their needs are met.

Children typically evolve from this place (and there are many young children who are incredibly conscious right from birth,) and some dogs can come in conscious and can also evolve.

Adults who are unconscious take everything at face value and question very little. They do not see or believe in anything beyond the physical plane. They oftentimes believe they are living the 'hand they were dealt.' Within this state of being, the experience of life isn't questioned. Life is what it is.

Conscious

The Conscious stage has several levels within it.

Preconscious

The starting stage of consciousness is a sense that there is something more, beyond what we know and what we can see. In this stage, a person can experience fear of the unknown, uncertainty and a feeling of looming or dread because they can always sense something beyond themselves but cannot identify it.

This often leads to questioning and searching. Some find the answers in religion, others break away from a religion when their searching pushes them to find answers beyond those provided through dogma.

Conscious

Stepping into consciousness is like unraveling a sweater. The more you search and question, the more what you think you know unravels. The difference is that when you finish your unraveling, you do not end up with nothing, you end up with unlimited possibilities.

We experience profound Trust and Faith that we are provided for and that we have the ability to create what we need and want. Our focus often shifts from the notion of God to the Universe and an awareness that we are a part of something greater than humanity, that there is something beyond being human and we search to learn how to create and manifest what we desire. We understand that life doesn't happen to us, but rather we are the creators of our own lives.

In a Conscious state, we begin to see the interconnectedness of everything, that there is a reason behind our life experiences, that life is something more than simply living, but yet life as we understand it, is simple.

We seek out guidance, answers, and direction to help us make sense of it all.

Awakened

In an Awakened state, we begin the process of stepping into full alignment with our own Spirit, and we recognize that the power to create our lives is within us and that our journey is to live as Spirit with a body. We come to understand that it is our Spirit that leads and guides us, and our physical body is the conscious vehicle through which our Spirit operates and flows.

As we step into this state we are given glimpses of what is possible when we live in this way. We are coaxed with the grace, ease, and flow that comes when we live as Spirit and are given examples of the gifts that come when we live as Spirit.

When I was living in upstate New York, I was renting this sweet little cabin near a pond. One morning, as I was meditating, looking at different things that were going on in and around my space. I was guided to take a journey to the Hall of Lessons on the Spiritual plane. When I arrived, I walked through the hall and noticed rooms and within each room was an Ascended Master, available for conversation. I visited with a few, Mary, Kwan Yin, Buddha, but it was Jesus that shared the most profound message with me.

As I sat with him he explained to me that his time on Earth was an attempt to show humanity what is possible when we live in a fully awakened state and when we live as Spirit with a body. As he demonstrated during his time, in this state, we can instantaneously manifest, our needs are immediately and always provided for, we can self-heal and heal others, we can transmute time and space and we have a direct connection to our divine source.

This wasn't the first time I got to hang out with Jesus. When I was a child, I had a dream, that wasn't a dream, a prophetic dream, a message. As I've mentioned I have had many like this since and the only way to describe them is that they have a quality, unlike a normal dream. They are tangible, they are real, they are clear, and they are easily remembered. In this dream state, I was in a Church (I was raised Roman Catholic) and it was empty, but I could feel someone else there. I approached the altar and as I did, Jesus walked out of the Vestibule and greeted me. He told me that there was more to life than this, that I was a bridge and that it was my purpose to uncover what this meant. I never told anyone about this dream and eventually forgot all about it, until I had this moment in the Hall of Lessons.

When I emerged from my meditation, it all made so much sense to me and was so clear. Of course, that was our journey—to grow from an unconscious state to an awakened state and in the process learn to live fully and completely as Spirit with a body, learning to embrace all of the powerful abilities that come with this state of being.

Simply, that is why we are here. To learn, heal and grow.

Spiritual Learning

It was through my clairvoyant reading space that I first began to understand how we learn our life lessons. Early on in my reading practice, over the course of a few weeks, I did readings for three different women. One lived in Delhi, India; one lived in Toronto, Ontario, Canada; one lived in the Midwest of the United States. They had different life experiences, different cultures, different family dynamics. They came from different religions; one was a stay-at-home mom, one was a professional woman and one was trying to figure out who she wanted to be.

As I moved through the three different readings, I started to see similarities—not in the details, but in the underlying dynamics. Each woman was working on her ability to live her Truth. The way the lessons were unfolding were unique, but the lesson was the same. As I reflected on these readings in my own meditation space and I recognized this thread the top of my head began tingling (my crown chakra—energy center.) A tingling crown chakra is one of my many messages from Spirit. This one lets me know that I'm tapping into something important for the Collective Consciousness and bringing in Universal Information.

I've spoken already a little bit about what I see as my true gift, and it is this ability to uncover, understand and share Universal Truths. I am so passionate about understanding the how, why and what-for of our lives and these three readings are what really got me started on this road. When I recognized that underneath the surface each woman was working on the same lesson, despite having such diverse backgrounds and lives; it fascinated me and intrigued me. I had questions! Was this a fluke, was it just this one lesson, were there others? How did we decide on what we were going to work? Or did we decide?

When I am looking at Spiritual information, I'll sit in my meditation space and search for the details. Sometimes I just let information flow, sometimes I take an experience or situation and I'll pull it apart energetically to see what it holds, to see what it is connected to, and to where it leads. It is a fascinating process.

I spent weeks looking at these questions around how we learn and the purpose behind it all. As the information expanded and settled into something that I could see and share, this is what I had gathered:

Universal Truth #1

Our primary purpose in any given lifetime is simple. It is to learn, heal and grow as Spiritual Beings.

That means that everything that we experience, and every relationship offers us an opportunity to learn something, to heal something and to grow Spiritually.

Universal Truth #2

As you grow, I grow. As I grow you grow.

Our growth is interconnected through the Spiritual agreements, or contracts, that we have with each other. Sometimes we are afraid to take the step that we are being pushed to take because we worry or have fear about how it will impact those around us. What I have learned is that we can equally and more deeply affect someone by not taking our steps. We can lock in place not only ourselves but also those we are in agreement with, by not doing our own Spiritual work and learning what we need to learn.

Universal Truth #3

All our life experiences, our challenges, those things that propel us to learn, heal and grow can be linked to four basic life lessons:

Stand in our Truth

Stand in our Power

Learn to Self-Validate

Live in Alignment

Here are some real-life examples. I asked the members of my Facebook group 'Awaken and Grow with Christine Agro' (www.facebook.com/groups/awakenandgrow) to share what they are challenged with in life. Here's what they shared, and I have boiled each challenge down to its corresponding life lesson.

Amanda: *Not having enough time.*

Although this was a bit of a winding road to get to the core life lesson at the heart of Amanda not having enough time, her core life lesson is Self-Validation. We fill ourselves with busyness in order to feel fulfilled and complete. Self-Validation is the answer.

Kayla: *Fear*

For Kayla, Living in Alignment is at the heart of the fear she experiences. When we live in alignment we are in the moment and when we are in the moment nothing exists but the moment, including fear. Fear can't exist if we are aligned. Living in Alignment is a 'next-step' Core Life Lessons. We only start to explore it after we step into learning consciously.

Jillian: *Acceptance*

Jillian is challenged with the acceptance of a certain situation. At the heart of it is Standing in her Truth. Her inability to accept what is, is fueled by not standing in the certainty of her Truth. Once standing in her own Truth, what is, is.

Lori: *Committing to Projects, Ideas, and Learning*

Where Lori had thought this was connected to Standing in her Truth, it was instead connected to Standing in her Power. Our Power is connected to our ego and our will. When we take a step to do something, to become something and cannot complete it or commit to it, we are afraid to stand in the full potential of who we are.

These are just a few examples of how we unconsciously work on our Core Life Lessons. As we move deeper and deeper into conscious awareness, we can start to see what our lessons are and how we are working on those lessons.

Universal Truth #4

The human experience has three states of being: unconscious, conscious and awakened.

As I shared already, there is nothing linear about this aspect of being. We can come in unconscious and leave unconscious. We can come in Conscious. We can grow to be awakened. But for the most part, once you step from unconscious to conscious; you can't go back. I say 'for the most part,' because I'm sure there are cases where someone has disconnected and returned to an unconscious state. I'm not one for 'absolutes.' There is no way that anyone can know everything about living, so I would question anyone who says, 'this is the way it is,' explicitly.

You Are a Point of Light

Many years ago, I sat in my meditation space and was guided to take a little journey above the Earth and was instructed to turn around and look back at it. When I did, I saw a grid around the Earth and on that grid a small smattering of lights anchoring the grid to the Earth. I understood this to mean that these were the beings anchoring in the current phase of conscious growth. I did not see many points of light and Spirit showed me that I was one of these points of light.

Many years later, I was guided to do the same thing and when I looked at the planet, the grid was full of lights and even as I looked at it, more and more lights were turning on. Each light represents a being stepping into consciousness. This second experience echoed what I was seeing in my teaching space: people were coming 'on-line' or stepping into consciousness in great droves and their growth was rapid. These people required a different process from the one I began teaching in the early 2000s and you are one of those points of light.

Take that in.

You are part of a movement, a Spiritual movement, of awakening, learning and growing.

AHAs

Did you have any Ahas or questions from this chapter?

Write them here and then join me over at my Awaken & Grow FB Group and share them. Your Aha or your question may help someone else (almost always does!) www.facebook.com/groups/awakenandgrow

Awaken & Grow Stories

Mudita Chandra, *CEO & Founder*

The Pure Experience

I knew about the concepts of right and wrong in navigating through life and I excelled at them, but it felt like there was a missing piece for me and I needed to look beyond, which I've found through the 3 concepts of standing in my truth, standing in my power and self-validation. I'm aware that I sought these from others and I can find these in myself which has freed me and at most times I have the awareness that the "issue" at hand is related to these three life lessons.

I have also gained awareness that I am an empath and greater understanding about my sensitivity. I am susceptible to the pictures others carry of me and how these pictures adversely impact what I can be, what I can do or what I can have. They affect my energy space and because I am a natural helper I end up taking on others growth periods and problems and make them my own. I have learned that when I do this, it adversely affects my own space which is generally filled with grace, ease, and flow.

I also have an intense need and desire to help animals. In India we have thousands of dogs and cows on the streets and it has been my life's work, commitment and heart's desire to help these four legged-friends lead better lives through my perspective as best as I am able. Awakening has hugely helped me to see what my animal friends require but also to not meddle in their soul's journey and to allow them their process and to support their choices and allow them to just be.

This level of awareness and shifts in perception have brought greater understanding and relief in my life. It has sharpened my ability to "see" things with more clarity and rather than seeing an unpleasant experience, interaction or situation as something that was happening to me and feeling a sense of powerlessness, at most times I am now able to see it as an opportunity to learn, heal and grow.

GROW

Once you take that step into consciousness, it is hard to go back and become unconscious again. Our growth may ebb and flow with different levels of clarity and focus. I see it with my students, quite often. They step into awareness by using a simple set of energy tools, then they stop using them and their clarity becomes foggy, then they make their way back to the energy tools and are reminded why using them and living awakened is so much easier. But it is all a part of our process of evolving.

The point is that our journey is rarely a straight line and every step back onto your path takes you deeper into aligning your physical reality with your spiritual truth. I frequently say, if you found a state of being once, you can find it again. Bliss, joy, alignment, however you experience it, isn't a one-time thing. If you experience it once, you can and will find it again.

Remember, the more you align, the closer and closer you get to living a state of aligned bliss that includes all of those abilities that Jesus shared with us—instantaneous manifestation, ability to self-heal and to heal others, the ability to transmute time and space and a clear and deep understanding of who we are, why we are here and what we are working on.

Now that you've had that 'aha' moment, that awakened moment, the questions loom, 'what's next and how do you move forward?' Certainly you could simply have the awakening and continue along with your life as it is, but I can tell you with almost absolute certainty, if you've had an awakening, you're going to keep being nudged by forces seen and unseen to open your eyes more and more, to connect more deeply and to take steps to align your physical world with a Spiritual reality that you may just be starting to acknowledge.

Why not make it easier on yourself and follow the signs, follow the nudges. Easier on yourself, because when we do not listen, the messages just get louder and louder until we have to listen until we have no other choice than to make the changes we are being asked to make. That is the 'Cosmic Correction.' When in order to hear the message, the correction is so loud, so big it feels like the carpet has been pulled out from under you. That doesn't have to be our process. Our growth can be easy, flowing, graceful, joyful.

Chapter 4

We never go backward.
Our growth is always forward motion.
You can't undo growth.
Christine Agro

How Do We Grow?

The Process of Spiritual Growth

I find it helpful when we are consciously growing, to have some understanding of the process, to have some awareness of how we actually learn. It is fascinating to look at our Spiritual process and once we understand how things unfold, the simplicity of it makes our journey so much easier. This 'how' is brought to you by countless readings I've done over the years, looking at what clients are dealing with and how and why it is showing up in their spaces, plus a smattering of my own personal learning. Rarely do I see something I haven't experienced myself.

In this chapter, I'm going to touch on three of the most common, confusing and frustrating experiences that come up when someone is stepping into consciousness. These three dynamics will make you feel like you are getting nowhere, but in truth, it is in recognizing them in your life, that lets you know you are truly growing. Each of these dynamics has not only entangled me during my own journey, but I have seen, I think it is safe to say, every student I work with deal with them in their own unique way. Some move through these dynamics quickly and others may sit in them for months or even years. On our Spiritual journey, there is no 'right' or 'wrong' way of growing. We grow in our own unique way and we have to learn for ourselves. In that vein, I share this with you, so you can, when you have the clarity to see it, understand your own growth process. That might be now, or this information may sit in reserve and one day, like the snap of a finger, you'll see it all clearly. Just remember, wherever you are in your journey is exactly where you are supposed to be.

Whether you can see your own growth process or not, another possibility is for you to start to look for these dynamics in others, because if you can see it in someone else, you can often learn what you wanted to learn by observation and move on to the next piece of your Spiritual lesson. That is a little shortcut you can use when you have conscious awareness. You can learn and then grow simply by observing how other people are doing their own work.

The three dynamics I want to introduce to you are The Spiritual Hokey Pokey, Ebb & Flow, and Layers.

The Spiritual Hokey Pokey

Do you know the children's' game 'The Hokey Pokey?' It is intended to help kids learn some of their body parts in a fun and experiential way. If you don't know it, it goes like this: Children stand in a circle and extend the mentioned body part into the circle and sing...

'You put your right arm in, you take your right arm out, you put your right arm in and you shake it all about, you do the Hokey Pokey and you turn yourself around, that's what it is all about it.'

As you move through the song, you put different parts of your body in and out of the circle you are standing in and 'shake them all about.'

I've defined an aspect of our Spiritual growth as our Spiritual Hokey Pokey. One possible stage of growth you may experience is the stepping into and back out of consciousness. You step into flow and back out of flow. For example, you find bliss and then you lose it again.

That's our Spiritual Hokey Pokey—we step on the path, we step off the path, we step on the path and that's what it IS all about it. Our Spiritual journey is about the process of learning, it is not about getting to a final 'somewhere.' On our Spiritual journey, the goal post is always moving. When you find that place of connectedness, there's another layer deeper that you can go. The deeper you go, the more clarity you gain, the more aware you become, the more you are able to channel the powers of your own Spirit. The more spiritual excavation you do, the more room you find to expand into who you are.

The challenge is, when we are learning and healing and growing, we can become frustrated because we had it and feel like we lost it when we step off the path. But here's the thing, this is an essential part of how we learn. When we are still in the Conscious expanding phase, we need to see the contrast between one way of living and another. It is in the noticing of that contrast that we begin to choose how we want to live, that we begin to understand that we do indeed have a choice. When my students say to me, 'oh, I had the most amazing moment, where I was totally connected, it was incredible, and then I lost it.' I always tell them, 'the beauty in this is that you found it once, know you will find it again.' These moments are opportunities to experience what our lives can be like when we live in an awakened, aligned state and an example of what happens when we choose to work on ourselves at this level.

I Wished I Hadn't Awakened

Once I wished I hadn't awakened. I had the thought that my life would be easier if I was still unconscious. I figured if I hadn't awakened, I wouldn't always be aware of my own growth process and wouldn't always be working through some aspect of my growth. As an aside, the truth is, whether you are conscious of your growth or not, you are always working through some aspect of your growth, but I was in a 'poor me' space, feeling like everything was so hard.

I'm fortunate that my Spirit chose a gentle way to show me what being Awakened afforded me. That morning, as I headed out the door for the day I heard Spirit whisper, 'don't forget your keys.' I stopped and looked and there they were on the kitchen counter. Had I not heard Spirit, I would have been locked out of the house as soon as I shut the door, with no easy way to get back in. I got in my Jeep and headed into town. I sped down the country road that we all frequently sped down, I was going 55 mph in a 40-mph zone and I heard, 'slow down, there's a cop up ahead.' As I slowed down to the speed limit, I rounded the bend to see the police officer with his speed gun in position. Next, I came up behind a Beet Truck full of sugar beets. The truck was so full that it was throwing off beets—big, hard beets. I'm a big fan of energetic bubbles for protection and always surround my car and home among other things with energetic bubbles. As I came upon the truck the beets were flying off and they hit all around me, but never touched the Jeep. I was able to pass the truck without getting hit by the beets. Once I got into town, I pulled into the market and parked. When I put the Jeep in park, I heard, 'move the car.' I did. I came out of the market to see another car in the spot I had been in and it was dented by the cart that had run into it. The entire day unfolded like this with me avoiding one mishap after another because I was awake.

Living life consciously doesn't eliminate challenges from happening, it means we have the tools, insight, and guidance to navigate those things in a way that others do not. It means we can move through life more effortlessly, but life still happens.

Ebb and Flow

I talk so much about Ebb and Flow my students have asked me to create a t-shirt. I talk about it so much, because when we understand that Ebb and Flow is a natural part of everything, that it is the rhythm of creation, then we can relax a bit not only when we are creating things, but also on our own Spiritual journey.

Ebb and flow. Think of the ocean waves moving in and back out. The tide flows in and then it ebbs back out. It is a constant process, a constant flow of energy. Never does the Ocean fear that when the tide ebbs, that it won't flow again. We can see this rhythm in the four seasons. We flow into Spring and Summer and then the energy begins to ebb, and we move into Autumn's harvest and then into the hibernation of Winter. But Spring always comes.

We can see this rhythm in the blossoming of a flower, flowing into its blooming state and then ebbing as its petals fade and eventually fall off, but the plant will have another bloom, when it is time.

When it is time!

That is the key to ebb and flow. All energy moves, when it is time. In our Spiritual growth, we ebb and flow through our life's journey. You have probably experienced this many times in your life. There are moments when everything is clicking, everything is flowing, life is moving along fluid and smooth, and then you hit an ebb. Movement forward slows, it may feel like you are stuck or even that you are moving backward. But you are not. When we move into a Spiritual ebb, we are allowing lessons to settle and healing to happen and we are preparing for new growth. We are gathering the energy, the tools, and the knowledge needed to flow forward again.

When we hit an ebb in something we are creating, it is a time to review what we have already created, assess its direction, confirm we are headed in the right direction. Given the time, space and breathing room, you will flow forward again. It is in understanding ebb and flow that we can find peace in our ebbs and learn to embrace them, maybe even enjoy them, for they are the pause before the next wave of life rushes into the shore.

If you are into Astrology, or you have ever heard someone shout, 'oh, no! It is Mercury Retrograde,' this is a built-in period of ebb in humanities otherwise ever pushing forward and unconscious way of living. Mercury in Retrograde happens three or four times a year and it is the time when the planet slows in its rotation and appears to move backward. When it does, its energy ebb has a direct impact on each of us, asking us to do anything and everything connected with the prefix 're.' Such as review, reset, reestablish, rethink, recollect, rewind, revisit, rebuild, reboot, and I could go on, but you get the idea. (If you are interested in finding out more about Mercury Retrograde, how it specifically impacts you and how to use it to deepen your own Spiritual connection, I've made a webinar available for you and it has a tracking sheet too! You'll find it in the Awaken & Grow Resource Bundle. The link is at the end of the book.)

Writing about ebb and flow brings to mind one of the most common places we try to push through the ebb, myself included, which is when we are looking for a job. In 1997, my first husband got a job in Denver, Colorado, so we decided to move. I moved there with him, without a job. I arrived in October and spent five months looking for a job in my field, and the whole time a voice kept saying 'enjoy this time,' but I couldn't. I could not relax into the ebb. I pushed and pushed against it as I applied and interviewed for different jobs. By March 1998, I had a new job, lots of responsibility and found myself up at 6 AM and home at 7 or 8 PM and thinking 'if, only I'd relaxed a bit during those five months.'

The ebb and flow of life are constant and a part of any act of creating. When we understand this, we can begin to better accept our own Spiritual growth process which often comes with its own ongoing experience of ebb and flow. Of course, the flow feels so much better, we are moving forward, things are happening, we see things coming into focus. The ebb can leave us feeling uncertain and uneasy, but when we understand what it is, we can stop pushing and step into the natural rhythm and allow our lives to unfold with ease.

Layers

We grow in layers and it's another place on our Spiritual journey where we can feel like we aren't getting anywhere. But the truth is, we work through one lesson, peel it off and underneath it is another piece to learn and another piece to heal. I'll talk a lot more about this in the next chapter, but I wanted to plant the seed here because it is part of the process of our growth. In the next chapter, I'll dive into what the layers are and how we acquire them.

When I work with students, the Spiritual Hokey Pokey, Ebb and Flow and Layers are the three most recurring experiences in our journey that create frustration. Now that you have an awareness of them, or maybe, more importantly, can put a name to what you've already noticed, when one or more of these experiences show up on your journey, you now know you are not alone and what you are experiencing is actually a part of your Spiritual growth. What can help is to not step into the 'picture' that you have slid backward or that you have made a mistake somehow, or even more importantly, that you have lost 'it.' Know that you are still learning, still healing and still growing.

AHAs

Did you have any Ahas or questions from this chapter?

Write them here and then join me over at my Awaken & Grow FB Group and share them. Your Aha or your question may help someone else (almost always does!) www.facebook.com/groups/awakenandgrow

Chapter 5

Change is the end result of all true learning.
Leo Buscaglia

Learn

Unconscious & Conscious Learning

We've looked at the stages and process of our Spiritual growth, but what about the actual way that we learn? This, I think, is some of the most important and helpful information regarding our Spiritual journey. The way in which we learn has stages too.

When we are unconscious we learn by being pushed, pulled and dragged along. Our lessons are learned not by choice, but by happenstance. We have an experience and if we do not learn the lesson, we create a similar experience to try to learn it and if we do not the pattern goes on and on and on. Life in this way can be magical or hell-on wheels as we careen through our days feeling out-of-control and experience life as a victim. We wonder 'why' things happen to us, and we wait in anguish for life to change, to experience flow in our lives.

Adversity

When we learn unconsciously, the only way we learn is through adversity. We need some form of pressure to get us to change, to get us to see the direction we are headed is wrong for us. Enter adversity.

Whether it is a relationship, your work, or your life habits, unconscious humans won't change unless something pushes us in a new direction. Remember early in the book, I spoke about 'Cosmic Corrections?' That is a loud, can't miss event that our Spirit sends us so that it is virtually impossible to choose to stay in your situation rather than accept the need for change. Adversity makes our lives challenging, difficult and painful.

However, when we step into consciousness we begin to understand there is both rhyme and reason to the things that happen. At this stage, we start to search for guidance and direction. We often speak of 'The Universe' as the force behind what happens, and we look for signs to help us make the right move and take the next step. We can still get caught off guard, forget we are in the driver's seat and hand over our power to others, but our conscious light draws us back to recognizing things happen for a reason.

As we move through learning consciously, at some point you read a book or you come to work with someone like me who changes how you see the world and how you see yourself within the world and that awareness puts the power of creating the life you choose in the palm of your own hands. And this is when we step into learning, healing and growing in an awakened state.

In this state, we recognize that everything that happens in our life is key to something we want to learn and heal so that we can evolve as a Spiritual being. We begin to search out information and search out tools and processes that can help us learn and heal, that make life simpler, more fluid and we begin to embrace the notion that what influences our life, isn't something 'out there,' it is not the Universe or something greater than ourselves, it is ourselves.

Over the years, I have fine-tuned a simple process that brings your learning and healing into an awakened state. The power to manage your own growth becomes yours. This process was introduced to me at The Inner Connection Institute, but as I worked with people and saw the changes in the ways that people were learning and growing, I began to adapt the process so that it best served where we are in our conscious growth. The Awaken Method is the product of almost 20 years and here's the thing, it continues to evolve, because we continue to evolve. What I share today, may not be what I share a year from now. In the Awaken & Grow Bonus Pack (link at the end of the book) you will find a video introduction to The Awaken Method.

Once we step into an Awakened state and have conscious awareness of how we learn, heal and grow then we can learn through many different ways. And this is one of the things about awakening that makes our lives flow. We can learn from our own experience, but we can also learn by watching others and observing what they are working on and how it is showing up in their lives. We can learn by watching a movie or reading a book or seeing something on television. I'll often get hooked on watching the same movie over and over and when I do, I know there is something there that I am looking to learn and understand about my own life lessons, something that once I see it, I can heal it within myself. The gift of this is having the ability to learn by observing others, we do not have to have the drama, trauma or challenge in our own life, we can simply see it, learn what we need to learn and heal what we want to heal.

The Process of Learning

Over & Over

How many times have you found yourself thinking, 'didn't I already deal with this? How am I back here AGAIN?'

I've already mentioned that we tend to learn our lessons in layers and how it is common to feel a sense of frustration when the seemingly same lesson keeps coming up over and over again. But it isn't the exact same lesson. It is a deeper layer and I'm going to explain why and how our lessons become layered.

Core Life Lessons

Here's how it works:

At the root of almost all of our learning are three basic core life lessons:

Self-Validation

Standing in Your Power

Standing in Your Truth

I play a game with my students and on call-in talk shows where I have people tell me what they are working on and I boil it down to one of these three core life lessons. It is incredible how at the root of everything are these three lessons.

Core Life Wounds

But here's what happens:

The first time we are faced with the opportunity to learn one of these lessons is generally when we are very young and unless we had conscious parents, chances are, we didn't learn the lesson at that point, but instead, we received a wound around the lesson.

Let's say your core life lesson is learning to Self-Validate. As a three-year-old, you went running to your mother with something and what you wanted was her to see you (validation.) A conscious parent would celebrate you and teach you how to validate yourself by saying something like; 'I'm so happy for you, you must be so proud of yourself!' But more likely, the parent isn't conscious and in fact is quite unconscious and instead of celebrating or even validating, the child is invalidated. Hence, a core life wound.

The child continues to experience life situations designed to help her self-validate which continue to result in invalidation, building layer, upon layer, upon layer of a core life wound.

As the child, now an adult, steps into Conscious awareness and begins self-healing, they are still learning unconsciously, and they begin the process, unknowingly, of peeling off the layers of the core life wound. That's why it can seem like we keep replaying the same lesson over and over again.

To step into working your Learning, Healing and Growing consciously; you need to look at these two things:

What core life lesson is at the root of whatever it is you are working on? (Hint, it can be more than one and sometimes all three behind a certain situation.)

At what point did the core life wound first appear.

Once you have these two pieces, you'll see how certain situations trigger that core life wound, adding another layer to it, and you'll begin to see just how many times throughout your life that core wound has led you to react and respond in particular ways.

Understanding that we learn and heal in layers, can greatly support you and even put your mind at ease as you navigate your Spiritual growth. Next time you feel like you're back where you started, consider that instead, you've reached a deeper layer of a core life wound and search for the core life lesson to which it is attached.

AHAs

Did you have any Ahas or questions from this chapter?

Write them here and then join me over at my Awaken & Grow FB Group and share them. Your Aha or your question may help someone else (almost always does!) www.facebook.com/groups/awakenandgrow

Awaken & Grow Stories

Lori Voss-Furukawa, *Founder of Create, Play, Grow*

Before I awakened my life was an emotional roller coaster filled with anxiety, insecurities, self-criticism and uncertainty.

I was often caught in the energies of other people. I was unable to stand in my own space and feel certain about who I was or what I was representing. I had a sense of independence, yet I was dependent on how others 'made' me feel. Conversations or things other people said would go around and around in my head, consuming my energy. I would look for support and validation from other people. When I didn't receive it, I would be crushed and frustrated. I was constantly looking for the approval of others.

I was uncertain of what I wanted in my life or who I wanted to be. My breathing was affected by my anxiety of so many things, mostly I worried about the future and what it would bring. Simple date nights or parties could trigger my anxiety. I came off as being independent and strong but inside I was out of touch with what was true to me. I was always trying to define myself by the standards that society was putting out there. Yet, deep inside I knew that there was more to life than what society, media or our culture tells us how to be.

Now my life is completely different, in a good way! I have control of what conversations go through my head. I now know that if something keeps coming back, it means I should look at it in my meditation space. I am so grateful for my daily meditation practice. It's by far one of the best tools that I have. But in saying that, I use so many tools in my meditation practice it's hard to have just one favorite.

I have learned to be grounded in my space, which helps me stand strong in who I am and what I am about. I tap into my certainty and instantly feel a sense of strength and knowingness within me. When I am unsure, it brings clarity and guidance into the situation.

I am so much more aware of what my body tells me now. If I notice my breathing is off, I know something is up, a trigger. Reminding myself to be in present time or to be in neutrality helps tremendously in keeping me grounded and stable.

Living an awakened life has no doubt enhanced all areas of my life. Having so many tools and the ability to use them allows me to move forward with grace and ease.

Chapter 6

Healing is an inside job.
Dr. B.J. Palmer

Heal

Learn. Heal. Grow.

The Healing part of this equation is where the work actually gets done. Many people stop at the learning, so I think this chapter is very important. We stop at the learning because we live in our mental body and the mind is trained to believe that as soon as it knows something that is all that is needed, but when it comes to our Spiritual growth, it is in the healing that we are able to move forward.

Why we have experiences

Have you ever wondered why things happen and how they happen? Is life random or is there some greater reason behind it all? I can tell you, there is definitely something deeper to the experiences we have in our lives. Our experiences are the vehicle for us to learn, heal and grow. Every conversation, every relationship, every moment holds an opportunity for us to move forward on our Spiritual journey.

It is through our relationships that our lessons unfold, whether that's our relationship with others or with things, like money, or with ourselves. Our lessons are wrapped up in our relationships. Through our relationships we have experiences; good, bad, indifferent. Within those experiences exists the lessons that we are trying to learn.

When we can understand this, it gives us the opportunity to consciously explore experiences and search them for the golden nuggets of learning that live within them. In the last chapter I shared with you our three Core Life Lessons: Self-Validation, Standing in Our Power and Standing in Our Truth. Every experience you have will have some element of your Core Life Lessons wrapped up in it. You will see either how you are learning it, or how it is challenging.

Let's take Standing in Our Truth as an example.

If we are working on Standing in Our Truth, our life experiences may revolve around different opportunities to be truthful to who we are and what we believe. We may find ourselves in a family that can't, won't or doesn't accept us for who we are. We may find ourselves challenged with the values of our workplace and needing to make decisions and choices that are at odds with each other (work or find another job for example.) In this case, it is through our life experiences that we will work on this Core Life Lesson.

Most people will work on the lesson but may never get to the healing part and that's because they are working the lesson unconsciously. Meaning, they are working the lesson without understanding what they are working on, why they are working on it or how they are working on it. This next piece is the key to creating a deeper connection with yourself and moving forward on your conscious path.

Healing comes by releasing

Healing comes not when we see what we are working on, but when we release what we are working on. We unconsciously create experiences that will 'light-up' or activate the energies we are trying to release, only we are taught from a very early age to push our feelings and thoughts down. Each time we do this, instead of healing by releasing what got activated, we add to the layers of our Core Life Wounds. We stack these moments one on top of the other and then we keep creating opportunities to activate the energies, but instead of releasing, we continue to push down that which we are trying to heal and create yet another layer.

How long it takes us to create that one moment.

Sometimes it can take a life-time or several lifetimes to build to a single experience during which we hope to get the healing we need to move our Spiritual awareness forward. That's why it is so very important to manage your own boundaries not only for yourself but in your interactions with others. It is important to make your own decisions. Similarly, if you are telling someone what they should or shouldn't do, you are taking away their opportunity to learn. I always recommend asking questions to help someone hone their choices, this allows them to make their own decisions, learn their own lessons and hopefully do their own healing.

AHAs

Did you have any Ahas or questions from this chapter?

Write them here and then join me over at my Awaken & Grow FB Group and share them. Your Aha or your question may help someone else (almost always does!) www.facebook.com/groups/awakenandgrow

Chapter 7

The key to growth is the introduction of higher dimensions of consciousness into our awareness.
Lao Tzu

Grow

I don't know if there is an endpoint to our growth. My sense is that we can grow infinitely and that as we grow, we gain greater clarity, certainty, and ability to see, understand and embrace ourselves as Spirits with a body. I think of our growth like a flower. We start as a bud and the petals start to open, one by one until we are in full bloom. I'm not sure what happens after we reach full bloom state. I feel like we have not gotten even close to that state. I'm not saying no one has fully bloomed ever, but it certainly isn't the norm for humanity. When I look at us clairvoyantly, I see that most of us barely begin to open in a given lifetime. Many never move past the bud stage. If you think about this, it is rather exciting because it means there is so much more for us to experience, so much more information and so many ways of being that we haven't even come close to touching yet. Another image I get when I sit with our Spiritual growth is that of a hall of mirrors that just keeps going and going. We are forever expanding and opening. As we step into conscious awareness, our growth keeps going and going and with each step we see more, know more and create more for ourselves. With each step, we deepen our connection to our own Divine Wisdom and Knowledge, to our own Spirit. We get closer to being able to channel the pure power of our Spirit through our physical body. As we continue to grow we create greater clarity, greater insight, greater knowingness and ultimately, we create peace, balance, and harmony within ourselves.

To recap, our growth comes about through our learning and healing. First, we need to see what we are working on, then we need to release the energies that are wrapped up in that lesson and then we experience healing which allows us to grow. The healing allows us to move to the next step in our journey. It opens the door to the next piece that will lead us to the next and the next.

During our initial stages of our conscious journey, we are peeling away the layers of our unconscious life. We are coming to understand what serves us and what doesn't serve us. As our growth continues we step into Conscious awareness and begin to understand our lives have a rhyme and a reason and we have more of say in how our life unfolds. At this stage, the more we grow the more conscious we become leading us to a state of Awakened being. At this stage, we have flow, alignment and our lives take on a new clarity. In our unconscious or evolving state we may think we are headed to a place of having it all, or a place where there are no challenges, but as you grow into your Awakened state what you will learn is that life is very different. In some ways, there are no words for what our lives become. Maybe because we move into a beautiful state of pure being and in this state, we have all we need to continue growing and evolving. It is, for me, the physical manifestation of a Bliss state.

In the next section, I share with you a collection of insights and tools that will help you to learn, heal and grow. The only thing I ask you to remember is that this work is experiential, it isn't meant to only be read and moved on from. It is in the doing that our true transformation happens. It is in the doing that we learn, heal and grow. Use the information in the next section as a stepping off point to embrace your own active growth and because I am so committed to helping you grow, remember that I have put together a resource bundle of 'doing' for you so you can take what you are reading here and put it into action. You will find a link at the end of the book where you can gather all of the resources I've created for you!

AHAs

Did you have any Ahas or questions from this chapter?

Write them here and then join me over at my Awaken & Grow FB Group and share them. Your Aha or your question may help someone else (almost always does!) www.facebook.com/groups/awakenandgrow

Awaken & Grow Stories

Radha Dumra *Knitwear Designer*

Before I awakened my life felt very constricted. I was born in a patriarchal family where no one saw my truth which led me to suppress my essence. That further led me to feel disconnected, lost and powerless. After working with Christine for several years my life has changed completely. I am now aware of all the dynamics in my family and relationships, where I can now look at it from a neutral space rather than getting pulled in emotionally. Instead of engaging their energy and seeking validation, I have learned to validate myself and have freed up so much space for who I am and what I want to be. I now have clarity on what is my truth vs their truth. I use many tools to manage my life on a daily basis. One which I love using is magnets and bubbles to clear the energy out. I feel empowered and connected my to spirit.

Putting It
All Together

So now what? You have a clearer understanding of why we are here and how we evolve as Spiritual beings, but for me that's just the stepping off point. The magic happens when we put it all together and when we have the tools to help us step into conscious learning, to deepen the connection to our own Spirit and to become active participants in our learning, healing, and growth.

In many ways, this book has unfolded in a similar way to how our Awakened state unfolds, gaining an understanding of something beyond what we knew and leading us into a place where we can apply that new knowledge. The third section may feel like stepping into another book because we can now look at the world and our lives through conscious eyes.

In this section we take all the concepts and put them into action. We see how, through our new perspective, we can create lives that we love. We see that we have the power to create true and lasting change and we come to understand how our own deeper growth helps us all to grow.

Chapter 8

Truth is ever to be found in simplicity,
and not in the multiplicity and confusion of things.
Isaac Newton

Keep It Simple

Simple Truths

Spiritual Truths and the energy tools that help us shift into Spiritual Awareness are simple. So simple that sometimes people find themselves thinking 'this can't work.' I know when people first start working with me, they are open to the possibility of change, but I can also see their questioning. But the proof is in the pudding, so-to-speak. Results speak volumes.

Universal Truths are those pieces of information that change the way we see and understand our own existence as it relates to the whole. Universal Truths show up in different guises, but underneath, remain the same.

I find someone like Carl Jung fascinating. Astrology was a basis for his archetypal structures and his exploration of 'the shadow.' What he did was make something that was unattainable attainable. He moved something that the mind couldn't fathom, into a realm of attainable knowledge. I also like looking at different religions and beliefs to see the similarities or the way in which Universal Truths show up in teachings and principles that inform a way of life.

Spirituality is simple. It is our mind that complicates things, but if we let our Spirit lead us, everything falls into place. When you find yourself struggling or feeling like you are pushing a boulder up hill, it is a good indication that your mind or your ego are running the show.

One of the many things I have learned over the years by doing readings for people is that our mental body is really limited. Severely limited. It can only conjure up ideas from that which it already knows. Yet it is the primary way most of us move through our lives, with our mental body guiding and directing us. Think of it this way, if your mental body only knows two possible options, you can then only choose between those two possible outcomes, but what if there are actually 10 possible options, 8 of which you have never experienced and so your mind cannot even begin to set you on those other 8 paths.

Our Ego is similar, only it drives us through needs and wants and a desire to be validated, to be acknowledged, to be seen and approved of. If our Ego is guiding us, we can easily get off our true path as we seek for something to fill us and tell us that we are 'okay.' The clarity, ease, and flow come about when we align with our own Spirit and we allow ourselves to be guided by our own higher-self, that aspect of us that knows why we are here, what we are working on and that aspect that holds the map of our life's journey. Retraining our mind and our ego to let Spirit lead can take some time, but the outcome is flow and ease and the unfolding of a life that you really can't imagine.

To circle back around to simplicity and to reiterate, Spiritual direction is simple. If you find that things are complicated or uncertain in life, that things aren't flowing; chances are, you are operating from your mental body or your ego body. In the light of 'simplicity,' shifting from chaos and indecision is simple; align with your own Spirit. When you use my simple alignment tool (I'm giving you another gift—you'll find a mini course in the resource bundle I've put together for you) the mental chatter stops, the spiral to find the right answer stops, you'll find quiet, peace and an internal balance. That all comes from aligning with your own Spirit and letting it guide.

Energy Work Works

When I work with students, I teach them energy tools to help create the change they want. Energy tools that remove energy, tools that release that which doesn't serve us, energy tools that connect us more deeply with our own Spirit. Again, it is our mind that tells us 'this cannot or will not work. I can't see it, therefore it can't really be doing anything.' Yet, this simple work has helped many, including myself, step from unconsciousness into a life of abundance, joy, and ease.

The difference between being awakened and creating a life you love rests, in my opinion, in having energy tools to help you navigate your life. To coin a phrase, 'the more you know, the more you grow.' Here's how a few of my students use their tools:

I use my tools to snap me out of a negative, "can't do" mindset. The grounding tools and the self-validation tool (gold suns) are my favorite. ~ Nadia

I use the grounding tool when I am having any sort of emotion that knocks me out of myself. I use the magnets and/ or bubbles a lot when I'm anxious or having intrusive thoughts, and I use the rose when I am rerunning an unpleasant moment with someone. These are the daily uses. ~ Hope

I use energy tools daily for a variety of things. Grounding and energetic and Spirit alignment to enable me to stand in my power and truth. Clearing other people's energy with magnets and using the rose technique to separate from others. The tools enable me to have clarity and certainty as I encounter different situations and people throughout the day. ~ Cappy

The Power of Energy Work

Energy work is so much more than internal work. What you do in your inner world, ripples out into the world around you and like anything that's aligned with your Spirit, Energy work is simple. Years ago, I met a scientist who got quite angry with me for talking about 'different realities' and where I understood his linear position that there is only one reality, when we work the energy of our lives, our reality and someone else's look completely different. When my life flows with grace and ease, when I'm in the right place at the right time; versus someone who's life is full of challenges and struggles, we, in fact, have 'different realities.' We could be walking side-by-side and our worlds are different. We experience our worlds (the same world, yet not) differently.

You might be asking yourself, 'well, if it is so simple to create a life we love, then why doesn't everyone?' Why do some people struggle, and others do not? I've touched on this earlier, but it comes down to what we are working on, what we are trying to learn and the roll that we are playing in this life. Which begs the next question, 'why would someone choose to play a role in which they are abused, or impoverished or disenfranchised?' It is not that someone chooses this consciously, but we need to go to the bigger picture to try and understand how life works. Which brings us back to The Collective Consciousness.

Remember that The Collective Consciousness is the source of all beings. I do this exercise with people where I have them raise their vibration so that they can rise up to the level of the Collective Consciousness to what I call, 'the sea of souls.' When there, we play with experiencing the Collective Consciousness, recognizing that

- we can be it and lose any boundary or barrier that differentiates us from the whole,
- we can be a part of it in a way where we see our boundary, but we are still part of the whole,
- we can move around it as an observer and
- we can stand in an individuated space of being our own unique Spirit where we still have a connection to the whole, but we are individual.

Before we are individuals, we are the whole and remember the purpose of the whole is to advance the collective consciousness in its journey of being. The way that happens is for individual spirits to incarnate into physical form (animal and human) and learn lessons that facilitate the growth of the whole.

When we first incarnated we came in to work on 1st chakra issues—issues of security, safety, stability. We were cave dwellers, we were nomadic, and our focus was on survival. As our collective growth evolved, we moved to second chakra issues—issues of emotions, sexuality and creativity. This time period includes discovery and creation—the wheel, tools, the ability to speak, it includes the Renaissance, the Industrial Revolution, and the Sexual Revolutions. If you're thinking, 'wow, that's a lot of time.' It is. Our evolution takes time. Interestingly, if you follow astrology, new planets and asteroids are typically discovered when we are taking steps into new areas of growth. Our more recent growth phase is connected with the 3rd Chakra and moving from an ego identity to a Spirit identity. This shift sees us recognizing that we are more than the physical form, that we are connected more deeply and that we have potentials we were disconnected from.

At any given time, incarnated Spirits can be working on any variation and combination of learning, healing and growing, but all of it is focused on moving the Collective Consciousness forward. So back to the question of 'why would someone choose a life of strife and challenge?' Incarnated, they do not. At Spirit they do because they want to learn something. In order to understand both extremes, we have to live both extremes. We have to live a life of power and a life of oppression. We have to live a life of wealth and a life of poverty. We have to live a life of faith and a life of faithlessness. For each of us, in every life, there is a light that we can fan or not. Will it take someone from poverty to riches, maybe, but maybe not. Will it make their life experience the difference between despair and hope? Absolutely and in that experience is the learning and growth.

If you've chosen to incarnate as an Empath, your path is to accelerate this process. In one single lifetime you will experience both extremes of the human condition. You will also learn by experiencing the life experiences of the people around you, those you know and those whom you have never met. If you live life this way, you can attest that this is not an easy way to move through the world. Stop for a minute and reflect:

Do you remember making this choice?

Does it make your life difficult?

Does it overwhelm you?

Anyone on the planet could ask themselves the exact same questions about the life they are experiencing but not everyone is at the conscious state to do that. What I know is that at Spirit we all have a plan for ourselves and it is not my or anyone else's place to judge or make assumptions about someone's life. The key is this: it is all of us that evolve the whole. If there are inequalities, it is those who see the inequalities who have the ability to create change, to educate, to empower, to provide healing and when someone steps up and says 'this isn't right, this needs to change,' or they say 'I see your pain, let me help you heal that,' we learn, we heal and we grow. Unconsciously, we live in a world of duality. Consciously, we live in a world of learning, healing and growing.

That is why the internal work that we do individually can have a ripple effect on the world around us. If you are awakening and stepping into consciousness, you are seeing things around you that do not match the truth you are embracing, and that experience creates change. If you are awakening and stepping into consciousness, you are opening up to having more and creating more in your life. As you wake up and create real change in your life, those around you take notice. Some will take their own steps forward, some will dig deeper into the life they are living to learn deeper. If you are awakening and stepping into consciousness you may only move your own spirit forward or you may spark a movement that creates change for many. The most important thing to remember is that pity or anger or resentment about someone else's life assumes that you know better than that Spirit and that your way of learning and healing and growing is more important and more relevant than theirs. Do not judge. See, understand and support. Do your own work, move into alignment with your own Spirit and your own Truth and let that ripple out to touch others in the way that is authentic and true for them. In other words, do not be a Spiritual Snob.

Animals helped me to see this so clearly. In 1999, I went to the Ann Wigmore Institute in Aguada, Puerto Rico to immerse myself in the Living Foods lifestyle. I spent three weeks there going through their program, learning to prepare Living Foods and focus on self-healing. While there I spent quite a bit of time wandering around the Island. It is a beautiful island, full of beautiful people. It is also an island with a large stray dog population. Puerto Rico's strays are called Satos, which basically means mutt or mongrel. At the Institute we were instructed to not befriend the dogs and told if we did, they would have to send the dogs to be euthanized. As I walked around the Island I saw packs of dogs. Many had wounds and poorly healed breaks. I asked someone at the Institute about some of the dogs and was told that people would 'break a Sato's leg to teach it not to go in their garbage.' Yet when I met the dog leader of one pack, carrying one of his hind legs tucked up in protection, walking strongly on three, he sat with me, let me pet him and despite being badly treated, was open to my companionship. It broke my heart to see these dogs. I found a local rescue and learned that people were helping the dogs, feeding them and sending those that could be adopted to the U.S. Mainland for adoption. I felt angry though. How could anyone treat a living being this way? When I returned to Colorado, I was doing some freelance grant writing work for The American Humane Association and one of the projects they put me on was The Link(C). The Link highlights the connection between Animal Abuse, Child Abuse, and Spousal Abuse. It was a call to first responders, social service workers, and medical providers to take note. If an animal in a home was being maltreated, chances were great that others in the house were also experiencing abuse. My recollection is that some of the research came from studies done with dogs in Puerto Rico. I saw the deeper link. The dogs of Puerto Rico, the lives they were living, helped bring to light an important indicator regarding abuse and abusers. Where they aren't conscious of this contribution, spiritually it is part of their journey to help humanity learn, heal and grow.

Microcosm | Macrocosm

I speak often in my work of Microcosm | Macrocosm—the notion that whatever we do influences the whole and what happens with the whole has an impact on each of us individually. As we learn, heal and grow the Collective learns, heals and grows. As someone learns the lessons of Success, the collective grows. As someone learns lessons of despair, the collective grows. If you subscribe to past-lives or ancestral lineage, we have all played the good guy and the bad guy. We've all been thieves and we have all been victims. We've been praised and shunned, we've been fruitful, and we've been barren.

Sometimes this is difficult for people to embrace, but it is the basis of the belief in Karma as well as Sin. We 'pay' for what we've done in the past. One action begets another whether in this lifetime or another. I like to think of it all without the guilt and shame though. It is Spiritual choice and it is necessary for our collective growth. Unconsciously, if we don't have something to fight against, to push back against, we don't do our deeper learning and our deeper growth. That is why it is so important to Awaken because when you do, you can stop learning your life lessons unconsciously. You can learn with conscious intent. You can see the lessons around you, rather than needing to unconsciously play them out. You can unravel your healing from within rather than needing to manifest a situation that evokes the healing you seek. That is how and why living an Awakened life helps you move to a life of grace, ease, and flow.

Moving from Unconscious to Conscious Growth

Challenge and Struggle vs Grace and Ease. You're ready to sign up for that, right?! A life without drama, where's the line form? It is all possible, but you have to say 'yes' to consciously unfolding your life lessons and actively stepping into the healing that will help you grow. Your life will become easier, not perfect. What I mean by that is this: Your life lessons do not go away, you still have things to learn, but the way in which you learn things shifts away from that antagonistic, duality- based tension that we see so much of around us. We are able to rise up and see the bigger picture, understand how the pieces of the puzzle go together, and we are able to learn and heal without having to have all of the drama or pain or confusion that exists for so many.

When we Awaken, we step into consciousness and with that, we step onto a path of conscious choice, and of spiritual exploration. Every experience, every encounter is an opportunity to learn something about ourselves and/or an opportunity to heal. Out of our learning and healing comes our growth. Out of our learning comes our expansion into more clarity, more balance, more time, more flow and simply, more.

Doing vs Reading

I know, you are reading this. We have to start somewhere. But our minds are tricksters, they convince us that we are 'doing' when in truth we are only amassing more and more information. If we do not do something with that information, if we do not embody it and become it, then we can read book after book on Spirituality and Spiritual growth and we aren't going to get very far. I had this awareness several years ago, when I started to explore this in readings and class space with clients and students.

I saw that although in the class space we would do the work, they were doing it with their mental body. In the class space they would understand it, but not really embody it. This kept students on the ebb and flow path of learning and healing. As I looked at this, I realized what was needed was to align with our own Spirits. When I first started exploring this with students, I'd ask them, 'when you look to your own Spirit, where do you look?' Most, if not all of them, would say above themselves. We were about to step into a huge shift. We began working on connecting Spirit and body, with consciously bringing the Spirit in and transferring all of the knowledge and wisdom that was gathered and stored in the Mental body, into the Physical body.

The first time I did this work on myself, I had so much energy I was awake for two days. The intensity of connecting Spirit and Body, of having Spirit fully and completely present in the physical form was incredible. Today, I continue to work with Aligning with Spirit and bringing the Spirit into the physical form, but what I find is that as a whole, this process is smoother, easier, and quicker. The same goes with other tools that I teach. What used to take students months to work through can now take weeks. Which takes me back to the point that the inner work each of us does has a ripple effect. When I started this work, we had to whack our way through the entangled weeds, where those arriving now, have a clearer path to follow, and far less weed whacking to do.

The key to deepening your Spiritual Connection rests in actually doing the work. You can read and read and read, but chances are you haven't been assimilating the information. You now need to marry all of that information you've amassed and transfer it, or download it to your physical form, to your body. That in itself is a powerful step in your awakening process.

AHAs

Did you have any Ahas or questions from this chapter?

Write them here and then join me over at my Awaken & Grow FB Group and share them. Your Aha or your question may help someone else (almost always does!) www.facebook.com/groups/awakenandgrow

Chapter 9

Going Deeper

Our Spiritual growth and evolution is as expansive as the universe and as deep as the Ocean. We cannot know the levels to which we can grow, nor can we see the depth of what we have to learn and heal. Many talk about our journey as something that has layers—onions, parfaits, layered holiday jello—whatever image you prefer, our growth consists of layer upon layer of learning and healing and deep at the bottom of each excavation lives a core life lesson. That core life lesson is the thing that you incarnated to learn and heal and through the process of peeling off the layers that is where our growth comes from. Each layer we remove gives us more space to be who we truly are. Each removed layer gives us more room to expand.

I was once asked if I was fully evolved? It was a curious question and one that made me stop and think. Not because I thought I was, but because I thought I wasn't even close. I see our potential to be as vast as the Universe. Remember 'microcosm / macrocosm?' I see each of us as our own starry Universe and when we step into conscious awareness, our Spiritual journey is like space exploration. When we acquire new insight, when we gain new tools it allows us to discover and excavate new places within us where we can learn and heal and that creates more room for us to expand and grow. It is like finding new galaxies within us.

Or if you've ever had a dream that you are in a house, maybe your house, and you discover a whole new area of the house you never knew was there? Dream analysis says, that dream is about expanding your sense of self, it is about finding an aspect of yourself you didn't know existed. It is a little trippy though to think about. We have the capacity to continue to learn something new about ourselves, the capacity to add a new level of ability and connection and it is always there. But we only get to begin to see it when we have a Spiritual Awakening.

Right now, with the information I have, I believe our growth is infinite. I do not think there is an 'end-game.' Or an end destination. I believe that we continue to grow as long as we are open to that growth. It is exciting to think about. The potential of who we are as Spirit with a Body has no limit, no boundaries.

For me, Going Deeper means that we say 'yes' to peeling away the layers, that we are open to exploring where there is no light, that we feel excitement about uncapping our unknown potential and that we take on the role of explorers in our own Spiritual Universe.

Captain of Your Own Ship

Most of humanity is not the captain of their own ship. Most people, in their unawakened state have life happen to them and when it does, they have little conscious control over what unfolds. Unawakened, we live in a reactive state of being. When we step into awareness, some people seek out a nirvana or a state of bliss or even enlightenment. What I teach is that enlightenment isn't somewhere outside of ourselves, it is within us. It isn't something to obtain or reach, it comes when we understand our life from a Spiritual perspective.

Our journey is to connect our Spirit with our body, so that it is our Spirit that is leading us and guiding us. Our mind, our ego, our emotions, our body, become the vehicle through which our spirit navigates us. It is when we connect and align with our Spirit that we become the captain of our ship. I remember when my Spiritual teacher said to me, 'Christine, one day you will be able to instantly manifest whatever you want.' Now, at the time, I thought that meant that I'd say apple, and poof the apple would appear in my hand and who knows, maybe one day I will be able to do that. But where I am at today is that I think, 'Oh, meant to get some apples,' and five minutes later my Mom walks in the door with a bag of apples. One could say that's just coincidence, and you're free to think that, but in my life, that kind of happening is common. I think it, I say it, and it manifests. For me, that's not coincidence. That's a result of being captain of my own ship.

Managing Your Growth

Going Deeper also gives us the ability to manage our own growth and manage our own Spiritual journey. I always say life becomes easier, it doesn't mean life doesn't still happen.

Take for example an exciting two weeks I had. It started with a relaxing afternoon at my favorite Float Bath, Zephyr Float which is in Kingston, NY. I left, felt great, stopped at a farmer's market, picked up some apples and a few other things. In the parking lot of the market, I checked my phone and saw 'Mom, you need to come home. A tree fell on our house.' What would your reaction be? What would you do? I took a breath, grounded myself and called home. My Mom was there as was my husband. Indeed a 100 ft Willow was on our house, and it was being taken care of. No one was injured, and the house was still standing. I continued home to the awe of this ancient tree resting on our house. As the week moved on, our Septic failed to the tune of $12,000; and a handful of minor emergencies arose requiring a shift in schedule and planning.

Without my awareness and The Awaken Method tools—grounding, centering, neutrality, connection to my own Spirit, the ability to clear energy and manifest my intention; these two weeks would have been hell. Instead, they were at worst, mildly annoying, and at best, they were part of the flow of life.

Awakening is the first step. But after you Awaken, there is so much more to gain, to learn, to do. There is a whole new way of living at your fingertips, but what you step into, depends on what teachers call you and what information you gain. For me, Awakening isn't just about waking up and recognizing that there is something more to living. Awakening is about turning life into something incredible and amazing. Turning life into an adventure that you get to explore and move through in the way that you choose to.

Growth Period

Our Growth unfolds as 'growth periods.' A growth period is when we are working on a specific spiritual lesson or working on healing something. The growth period is comprised of all the things we experience that are either trying to help us learn the lesson or have the healing. If we are unconscious or unaware our growth periods are typically times of confusion, anxiety, stress and uncertainty. They might be connected to our relationships, or our work life, or our family life. They can be connected to our safety and security. Without tools and an understanding of what we are working on, our life can seem out of control or overwhelming. We may be wondering, 'what's happening to me?' and we may feel like our lives are falling apart. When we have awareness combined with energy tools life moves from something that happens to us and around us, to something we can navigate, something we can shape and something we are an active part of creating.

I teach *The Awaken Method* as a starting place. It is a core group of energy tools that come together to provide a simple daily practice. The core tools include learning how to ground, how to align with your own Spirit or higher power, how to sit in a space of neutrality, how to define and hold your energetic space and how to replenish yourself and empower yourself. Once you learn the core tools, I am a tool maniac. If you've got something going on, or I see something in your space, there's a tool to help you explore it, manage it, shift it, clear it, or transmute it. Beyond the Awaken Method, people who work with me learn how to explore everything from the growth periods they are in, to their core life lessons, to how to energetically set up and manage their relationships, how to manifest what they want, and basically how to 'work' the energy of any experience or situation, because at the end of the day, everything is comprised of energy and everything can be worked with on an energetic level.

I want to spend some time here introducing you to four of the seven core tools and giving you a few exercises to do so that you have tools to help support you on your journey.

Tools to Support You

What I'm sharing with you here are four of the core tools that come together as part of *The Awaken Method*, a simple daily process to help you manage all aspects of your life and create what you really want. I have a free quiz you can take to see which tool you need most, and I encourage you to check it out. You'll find a link to it in the Resource Bundle. Individually, these tools can really support you on your Awakened journey, however, when you combine all of these tools into a single daily practice, they become exponentially more powerful and supportive for your personal growth.

Years ago, before I started this work, I used to joke that I'd like to have a Spiritual Life Manager, a guide to whom I could ask any question about my life and get the direction and insight I needed, someone to take all the guessing out of what to do and when to do it. As I was contemplating the information for this book, I realized that I finally manifested that person and that it is me. Through this work, I have become my own life manager. When I live with and through these simple tools, everything I need to see, to understand, to step into, is clear.

Grounding

I like to look to Nature for insight and guidance, because Nature is pure Spirit. When it comes to being connected or grounded, Nature certainly has some great examples and lessons for us. The ability to root down into the earth, to connect more deeply and provide a stable base from which we operate is the key to creating balance, stability, peace and even flexibility. Although creating flexibility by rooting ourselves may seem counterintuitive, grounding does create flexibility because we can function from a solid core that allows us to bend, move and shift when needed, without feeling like we are spiraling or out of control.

How to Ground

Grounding, like all of my tools, is simple.

To start, sit in a chair with your feet flat on the floor.

Close your eyes.

Take a breath in and out.

Now, see or intend or pretend that you are sending or growing roots from your feet down into the earth.

It is that simple. The more you practice this tool, the more grounded you become which ripples out into your everyday experience.

Grounding, like everything I teach, has layers and levels to it and those layers and levels are connected to your own Spiritual growth and journey. The more you learn and heal, the deeper your growth is, the more conscious you become, the deeper your Spiritual connection becomes. Let's think about Nature again. If you've ever pulled a weed from your garden, you know that some roots are thin and wispy, and some go so deep and anchor in so strongly that it takes great force to uproot the plant or tree they are attached to.

As you explore Grounding, you may find that your roots change over time or even from time to time. When I teach in person or give an experiential talk, I often have people do a fun grounding exercise toward the beginning. I have people pair up with one person standing behind the other and then gently move the person in front by placing their hands on their shoulders and pushing the person front to back, side to side. And then we repeat the process after they have grounded. This is a great way to understand first how simple this work is and second, how effective it is. Inevitably they notice anything from more stability to more connectedness, while experiencing a great sense of freedom and even certainty.

For a little fun, I typically have someone from the group try to move me. Because I have been grounding for so long (almost 20 years now,) I do not move very much, which always surprises everyone, because my nature is so 'go-with-the-flow.' That's just another example that being grounded doesn't mean stuck or inflexible, being grounded provides strength, connection, and a strong place from which to grow.

How Does Grounding Benefit You?

Grounding, like the tree, provides a connection to the earth. When you are grounded, it sends a message to the body that it is safe. In Yoga, one of the eight limbs is to see the body as the vessel for our Spirit. That's great, but the problem is that, for most of us, our Spirit doesn't inhabit our body, it hovers outside of our body, waiting for us to reach a level of conscious awareness and create the space for Spirit to connect with the body. Remember this connection is core to my work—helping you connect your body to your Spirit, because it is Spirit that has all the cool bells and whistles, but without the body as the vehicle, we have no way to play with them—things like the ability to instantaneously manifest, access to our higher senses, the ability to transmute time and space and the ability to heal ourselves and others. Learning to ground, to root your body into the Earth, while retaining flexibility and flow is the starting place for connecting your Spirit with your body.

Neutrality

Neutrality is the ability to 'not engage' the energy. It offers us a place of clarity to move through our lives and is a powerful tool that helps us navigate the world we live in and the people we encounter. When we have the ability to 'not engage' the energy, we keep our personal power, we keep our energy, we choose what and to whom we respond. Developing neutrality offers both true freedom and true personal power.

Take this example: Your mom (substitute brother, best friend, co-worker—you get the point,) seems to always hit you with the same kind of criticism that just sends you over the edge. You end up feeling like a child and like you are inferior and incapable of living your life. Not a conversation passes that you do not come away feeling less-than. But you can't seem to step out of the cycle and your mom always manages to zing you. When you develop neutrality, you gain the power to 'not engage' her zings. They no longer hit you in your heart, or your solar plexus or your throat. Instead of hitting their mark, they fall flat. It takes time and practice to develop neutrality and I have a unique way of teaching you how, but in short, if you simply prepare yourself before the call or the gathering with the conscious thought of 'I'm not going to engage the energy,' you'll begin the process of developing neutrality.

Alignment

Alignment is the cornerstone of my Spiritual growth toolbox. I mentioned that in Yoga the body is seen as the vehicle for our Spirit, but without a way to connect the Spirit, without a way to clear that which keeps us disconnected, Spirit lives outside of us. Alignment is one of the most powerful tools because it helps to facilitate that process of connecting our Spirit and our body. When we step into alignment, we are aligning with our own Spirit. We are putting the mind, the ego, the emotions and the physical body into alignment with our own Spirit. We are consciously releasing those aspects of ourselves from needing to be in control and acknowledging that it is our own Spirit that has our life's game plan. It is through aligning with our Spirit that life truly begins to flow.

How to Align

Sit in a quiet place with your feet flat on the floor.

Close your eyes and take a breath in and out.

Imagine, pretend or intend that you have a beam of light that connects from the base of your tailbone to the top of your head, that runs straight through the core of your spine.

With your intention, intend that you come into energetic alignment with this beam of light.

Practice this daily.

In your Awaken & Grow Bonus Pack, I have provided you a short video that walks you through this introduction to the Alignment tool—it is another free gift to help support you on your Awakened Journey.

Clearing

Think of a house with every shelf and every closet full of things you've acquired over the years. Maybe you have so much stuff that your attic is full, as is your basement and maybe you have an extra storage like a garage or a shed. Maybe, you even keep stuff in your car.

That's what we are like, full of energetic clutter and stuff that we've stored away, just in case we might need it someday. All of that stuff, those thoughts, those words, those experiences, all of that stuff takes up space and displaces our own Spirit. Add to this, if you are energetically sensitive you are like a sponge, soaking up the emotions and experiences of the people you know and even of those you do not know.

Needless to say, a simple tool to help you 'Clear the Clutter,' can be a total life changer. Learning how to energetically clear your space and then fill in with the energies that we choose to be full of, shifts how we not only experience our days, but also how we experience ourselves.

How to Clear the Clutter (or a place to start)

Sit with your feet flat on the floor

Close your eyes

Take a breath in and out.

Imagine a powerful magnet or an energetic vacuum cleaner and use it to clear the energetic clutter.

When you finish, set your intention to fill yourself in with your highest energetic vibration.

In the Awaken & Grow Bonus Pack, I have given you access to my five part course called 'Clear The Clutter.' It will take you much deeper than this simple place to start.

Creating Real Change

At the beginning of this chapter, I said that you might think this is just too simple to actually work. But the truth is, with almost 20 years of watching people create real and lasting change in their lives, these tools work. If you create a simple daily practice and combine the four tools I've shared with you here, your life will change.

AHAs

Did you have any Ahas or questions from this chapter?

Write them here and then join me over at my Awaken & Grow FB Group and share them. Your Aha or your question may help someone else (almost always does!) www.facebook.com/groups/awakenandgrow

Awaken & Grow Stories

Cappy Caporuscio,

Mechanical Engineer & Founder of Upshift

Before awakening, I found myself living the 'When I…' life—when I find the right job, when I find the right man, when I whatever, my life will be wonderful. I was always searching, overthinking, striving to find a sense of peace in my life. I spent so much of my time being extremely hard on myself for not being, doing or having what I thought I should at any given time in my life. I didn't know it at the time but the 'When I' I was chasing was 'When I find Christine'.

Throughout my life's journey, I secretly read books about enlightenment, awakening, New Age, etc. I rarely, if ever, discussed my interests in these areas with anyone—my technical training and upbringing did not allow for the existence of anything other than what I had been taught. And, enlightenment seemed like something that would be unattainable for me; I was no one special. Even if I decided to try, it would be a long journey from where I was to where the people in the books seemed to be. My choices and behaviors were most certainly not those of what I pictured an enlightened person to be. I tried to ignore the urgings to learn more and managed to successfully squelch them, or so I thought. The more I tried to ignore or push away the thoughts or events that were pushing me towards it, the more I was compelled to pursue it. The strongest push came in the form of a Chocolate Lab named Maxx.

Maxx was the love of my adult life and my saving grace, coming to me at a time when I was spiraling in so many areas of my life. His presence in my life kept me grounded. Just knowing that I had Maxx to take care of gave me the thread that led me to the path of awakening. During our thirteen and a half years together, Maxx blessed me in so many ways, but his biggest legacy was leading me to Christine.

Maxx's health started to decline when he was about eleven and a half. Despite having a wonderful vet to consult with on an almost daily basis and easy access to one of the top vet schools on the east coast, the cause of Maxx's illness was difficult to diagnose and the conventional medicines he was given were causing more issues for him. I was desperate to do the right thing for him, to get him any help I could find but I had no idea what to do or where to turn. But something deep inside me urged me to search for something else, something more, something beyond what I knew and what I was being told.

My mind was still fairly closed to unconventional treatments, but I was determined to help Maxx, whatever it took so I started to search out options. I had *experienced essential oils at the neighbor's house once and was intrigued by them. I was open to the possibility that maybe they would help Maxx – they had somehow become okay in my mind. The internet was just starting to take hold, so I decided to search for someone who could help dogs with essential oils. The internet led me to Christine. Through her amazing knowledge and skills, Christine was able to help me understand what was going on with Maxx physically and emotionally and, with her help, his health improved, and we were blessed with more than two additional healthy years together.*

It has been 10 years since Maxx transitioned. His presence in my life opened the path for my awakening and, in honor of him, I made a choice to stay on that path, being more open to things that may not initially align with my current belief system or knowledge. I have remained in contact with Christine for thirteen years, taking many of the courses she offered and applying the knowledge she shared.

Today, I lead a much more conscious life, looking at my life events and situations as growth and learning opportunities, seeing and understanding the deeper meaning of their presence in my life, and releasing things that don't belong to me or no longer serve me. By utilizing the tools Christine has shared over the years,

I am able to align, easily see my path and make choices that support my journey.

The greatest gift I have received is the ability to navigate life with grace and ease, choosing how I want to live, consciously and with intention.

Chapter 10

'The desire to know your own soul
will end all other desires.'
Rumi

Create a Life You Love

What is it we all want and need in our lives? Love, safety, know-ing that we have what we need, that everything will be okay., peace, balance, ease. There are many ways to try to achieve these things or bring them into our lives, but the most successful and complete way is to connect more deeply with your own Spirit and with your own Spiritual journey. As you step into your awakened state and begin to see your life as an opportu-nity to learn the Spiritual lessons you came here to learn, and heal the things you wanted to heal, you begin to create a life you truly love. Even if you already think 'hey, my life is good already,' when we take this step, life becomes so incredibly rich and rewarding. We move from a place of life happening to us, to a place where we can manage and navigate the things that come up in our lives with a sense of grace and ease and in many cases, with amusement, and from a place where we can create what we want.

What Can You Do Once You Awaken?

Let's spend a little bit of time exploring what you can do once you awaken, because the more connected you become to the Spiritual flow of your life, the more amazing, wonderful, cool things you can do in your life.

Understand Your Life Lessons

When you can see your life lessons it helps you make sense of how your life flows and how you experience your life. We've already explored the four core life lessons. The things we experience in our lives can all circle back to these four lessons: Learning to self-validate, standing in your power, speaking your truth and living in Spiritual alignment. The last, living in Spiritual alignment, we get to only after we understand the first three and how we work on them in our lives.

One of the most common reactions to this piece is that this makes one responsible for what has happened to them during their life. Possibly, it takes really being awake to understand that this is not what is meant by this at all. No one consciously wants to have horrid things happen in their lives, or experience a disease in order to learn a Spiritual life lesson, but when we live life unconsciously, the only way we can learn and grow and truly experience life is by having life experiences that challenge us, that push us and that make us look at who we are and how we move through the world. We cannot look at this principle from the physical world perspective because if we do, we cannot understand it.

Yet at the same time, many have no problem accepting the notion of Original Sin and its process of absolution or accepting the notion of Karma. Each of these does apply a physical world 'fault' on the individual, whereas the Spiritual notion of understanding what we are working on does not assign fault. It simply explores what lessons rest at the core of our life experiences. If this challenges you, I say, 'good,' because that means it is poking at something for you to look at, something for you to explore.

Often when something doesn't make sense, or you just can't seem to comprehend the meaning or connection behind something, there is a deep piece of learning attached to it. Once, someone began speaking to me about 'duality.' I felt so uncomfortable and even a bit confused. I sat for a while with the conversation and kept rolling the word 'duality' around in my mind, saying it, writing it. I just couldn't connect with the word. I finally looked up the definition to see if that would help with my confusion. When I read the definition I said to myself, 'oh, I see, I do not actually believe in duality. That's why this made no sense to me.' I use this tool regularly now. When a word seems or feels foreign or out-of-this-world, I look it up and generally glean something about myself. But the short is that this is exactly what I'm talking about regarding our life lessons. If you are feeling uncomfortable about our life being about our lessons and our lessons being learned through our life experiences, maybe there is something more there for you to explore? Maybe, it is Spirit calling you to look at your life differently?

If you are already in alignment with this information, then the question to you is, 'what have you been working on and how is it showing up in your life?' It is this essential next step that moves your Awakening from just an 'aha' or a powerful moment, into a whole new way of living your life.

Manage Your Life Lessons

We're talking about Spirituality 2.0 here. About moving from Awareness to actually doing something with that awareness, that's the GROW part of all of this and that's what makes my work different. It is not just about waking up, it is about understanding what you can do and having the tools to actually do something with your awakened state which enables you to live an empowered life.

I was working with a client the other day and we were working with Neutrality. As I walked her through the tool, she said, 'oh, that's like the 5th Dimension in the work that I've been doing.' Using my clairvoyance, I could see that the spaces looked similar if not the same, the difference is that I explained how to use the space. It wasn't just a space to 'go to,' or a state to achieve, it is an actual and practical space that can be used in your day-to-day experiences that helps you to not engage the energies you encounter.

Clear, Heal and Release Old Information

This is a huge, huge, part of spiritual growth. As children, we are taught to push our emotions and fear and pain down. We are taught to ignore it, to stifle it, to shut it down. But those experiences are the fuel for learning our life lessons. Every time we shut these moments down, every time we bury them, we build a layer around the core life lesson that those experiences were pushing you to learn. In turn, we end up spending our life experiencing moments meant to help us learn our core life lessons, resisting them and struggling with them. When we are Awakened, and we understand the lessons we are working on, we can begin to learn our lessons consciously. We can learn our lessons by seeing others' work through their own lessons, we can also learn to see our own lessons and unravel the layers, so we can learn the lesson and evolve.

And most importantly, rather than push those experiences down, we can raise them up and clear them out and take a step in our Spiritual growth.

Consciously Manifest

As we deepen our connection to our own Spirit, we uncover and learn to use our ability to consciously manifest all that we want in our life. It can be a fun ability to play with. When we first start playing with our ability to manifest, we oftentimes go for the big things, 'I want a million dollars,' or 'I want to take a trip around the world.' Certainly, these are things you can manifest, but it is important to know that just like uncovering our life lessons, developing our ability to manifest what we want comes with lessons to learn and healing to do. When we ask for a million dollars, we set in motion the work that we need to do in order to have a million dollars. Think about this. What exactly do you need to learn and clear to have one million dollars? Additionally, most often, our lack of money is connected to other lessons we are learning. If we had the financial stability, we would stop growing and not learn what we intended for ourselves.

In order to manifest instantly, we need to uncover, release, clear and heal anything that is in the way of us having this ability. Without the development of our conscious awareness and our healing, we have the potential to manifest things that we do not really want or to cut our Spiritual growth short. The learning period helps us peel away the layers that clutter our clarity when it comes to what is in alignment with our true self.

Play with Time

As we move into Awareness, we start to experience the 4th dimensional energies of time and space and a month can seem like a day and a minute can seem like hours.

When I was living in the Adirondacks in Upstate New York, one Sunday morning I was leading a workshop on Animal Communication in a town that's normally an hour drive away. I woke up to four feet of snow and my Jeep completely snowed in and all I had was a shovel. I was certain after shoveling the Jeep out and being only able to drive 35 miles an hour on a 55 mile an hour road that I would be late. As I drove, I centered myself and used my simple energy tool to stretch time. The tool is beyond simple. You place your palms together and pull them apart with the intention to stretch time. Not only did I get there on time, I was ten minutes early, going 35 miles an hour. You can use this tool to condense time as well, you just reverse the process.

Practical Spirituality

Practical Spirituality is the act or art of bringing your Spiritual practice into your everyday living. You can sit in meditation or spend time doing yoga but if you leave your bliss on your mat, you're really just escaping from the day-to-day through your Spiritual practice. As you have read, I believe that true change comes when we have practical tools to help us deepen our awareness and to expand our experience of living as a Spiritual being in a physical body.

Now that you have a basic understanding of the process we go through when we Awaken, the potential it holds for your own deeper life experience and tools to help you grow, the choice is yours and the choice is part of your Awakening. What will you do next? That's one of my favorite questions because it is open ended and full of possibility and opportunity. It is time to step into your childlike wonder and explore the depths of who you are, what you are working on and where you're understanding of your own life lessons will take you.

How Does Your Life Change?

When you Awaken, your life becomes easier. It doesn't mean that you don't or won't experience challenges, but once you awaken and you understand how your life and life in general works from a Spiritual perspective, life becomes easier.

Not only will you acquire the ability to manage the way you move through your life, but you also develop the ability to truly create what you want in your life.

From relationships to what you have and what you do. This is what is meant when people talk about 'life flowing.'

Final Words

As you take this step into living a conscious life, I encourage you to keep the following in mind:

Live in Amusement as it will create a natural grace and ease in your life.

Live in Alignment as it will ensure you stay on your true Spiritual path.

Live with an open heart and open hand, as giving and receiving create a true infinity loop and to have all that you desire, giving and receiving must flow freely and fully.

Live with a sense of wonder. Tap into your childlike curiosity and find joy and excitement in unraveling the mysteries of your own life.

Thank you so much for spending your time with me and I hope this book has caused more than one 'aha' moment for you. You're on your way to living a life you can't even dream of at this point, because your mind can only know what it already knows. What you are creating is based in the unlimited expanse of living a life as an empowered Spiritual being.

I'm so excited for you!

AHAs

Did you have any Ahas or questions from this chapter?

Write them here and then join me over at my Awaken & Grow FB Group and share them. Your Aha or your question may help someone else (almost always does!) www.facebook.com/groups/awakenandgrow

Awaken & Grow Bonus Package

Please visit www.AwakenandGrowBonusPack.com to receive your *Awaken and Grow Bonus Package*

You will find:
Awaken Method Intro
Mini Course on Alignment
Mercury Retrograde tracking sheet and tutorial
14 Day Present Time Challenge
5 Day Clear the Clutter Program

Awaken & Grow Facebook Group

Join me here:
www.facebook.com/groups/awakenandgrow

About Christine Agro

Christine Agro is a Spiritual Teacher, Clairvoyant and a noted Spiritual and Metaphysical Authority. She has been channeling the Collective Consciousness for almost 20 years and sharing simple Universal Truths.

Christine promotes practical Spirituality that is rooted in our day-to-day lives and that facilitates real and positive change.

Christine has been featured in the *New York Times* and *Vogue Japan*, seen on *The Late Show with Seth Meyers*, and *Animal Planet* and is cited in several books including Grace Coddington's New York Times Best Selling book *Grace: A Memoir*, *Super Natural America*, by Lawrence Samuel and *Messages from Spirit*, by Colette Baron-Reid (Hay House.)

Christine is also author of *50 Ways to Live Life Consciously: 8 Energetic Tools and 42 Concepts to Help You Wake-Up and Live* and the *Nature Inspired Anthologies*.

Christine helps women create positive change in their lives and step into Conscious Living and Conscious Learning through group programs, one-to-one deep dive mentoring, through her Awaken & Grow TV show and through her various projects like her Tuesday #consciouschat Twitter Chats.

Join Christine here:

www.facebook.com/christineagro

www.twitter.com/christineagro

www.youtube.com/user/christineagro

www.instagram.com/christineagro

www.pinterest.com/christineagro

www.linkedin.com/in/christineagro

Website:

www.awakenandgrow.com

Contact Christine via Email:

learn@awakenandgrow.com